iBloom *in* BUSINESS

EQUIPPING YOU TO BUILD A SUCCESSFUL BUSINESS WHILE LIVING A LIFE YOU LOVE!

Kelly Thorne Gore

Lexington, KY

www.ibloom.us

iBloom in Business: Equipping You to Build a Successful Business While Living a Life You Love!

Copyright © 2013 by Kelly Thorne Gore

Published by iBloom, LLC
Lexington, KY 40555
www.ibloom.us

Requests for information should be addressed to:
iBloom, PO Box 55131, Lexington, KY 40555
info@ibloom.us

Unless otherwise indicated, all Scripture quotations are taken from the HOLY BIBLE, NEW INTERNATIONAL VERSION®. NIV®. Copyright © 1973, 1978, 1984 by the International Bible Society. Used by permission of Zondervan. All rights reserved.

Verses marked with MSG are taken from The Message. Copyright © Eugene H. Peterson 1993, 1994, 1995, 1996, 2000, 2001, 2002. Used by permission of NavPress Publishing Group.

ISBN: 978-0-9826626-4-9

For the iBloom Team:

Jane Thorne, Lori Burrell, Betsy Ringer,
Leigh Ann Napier, and Amanda Taylor

Thank you for partnering with me on this incredible ministry journey. I'm so honored and blessed to serve alongside you.

Acknowledgements

Lord, thank you for entrusting this gift to me. Thank you for the life experiences and lessons that made this book possible. I pray that You use it, as You see fit. Thank you for loving me and being the best business partner a girl could have!

Jon, I'm so grateful that you're finally in my life. I can't thank God enough for you and the amazing man you are. You were definitely worth the many years of praying, preparing, and waiting. Thank you for believing in me and supporting me through each step of this journey. I'm so honored to be your wife and best friend.

Mom & Dad, this project is possible because of you. Thank you seems so inadequate to express my gratitude for your many years of support, encouragement, and unconditional love. You always instilled in me that I could do anything and then you tirelessly supported each endeavor I pursued. I'm so blessed to have you as my parents.

Chris, thank you for being such a great brother and friend. Your willingness to serve wherever you're needed is a HUGE blessing to me and so many others. I'm SO grateful for YOU!

Sherry and Mark, I'm so blessed to have you as my family. Thank you for all that you do behind the scenes to support me.

Diane Cunningham, thank you for being my business sounding board for so many years. Many don't understand us, but I'm so grateful that we have one another. I'm so proud of you!

Mentors, I've been so blessed to have many life and business mentors who have come alongside to support, encourage, and challenge me. Thank you for investing in me and my growth!

Clients, thank you for being the guinea pigs that allowed me to test out all of this material.

There are so many more people that I want to thank, but how on earth can I say thank you to the countless people who have positively influenced my life? It would literally take pages upon pages. One thing is for sure -I'm SO incredibly blessed! THANK YOU!

Contents

Scan this QR code using your smart phone or go to
www.ibloom.co/business-book-resources for an online
library of resources to accompany this book.

Free Gift for YOU!
One Month FREE in our
iBloom in Business Inner Circle

The iBloom in Business Inner Circle is the best way I can partner with you and your business, so you can successful implement each step that you will learn in this book.

Benefits to the Inner Circle include:

- Weekly Video Teachings where we dive deeper into each of the concepts from this book,

- Monthly Q&A Session where you can get answers to your questions, receive accountability, and encouragement,

- Plus, you have the added benefit of encouragement, support, and collaboration opportunities with members in our private Facebook group.

Scan this QR code using your smart phone or go to www.ibloom.co/businessinnercircle to sign-up for the iBloom in Business Inner Circle. Your first month is my gift to you, so I can personally give you accountability and support as you implement all that you will learn in this book. Just use the coupon code: **success** at checkout to receive your discount. This is a month-to-month coaching program, so you can cancel at any time.

Introduction

Hi! I'm SO glad you've picked up this book. I assume that since you're reading this book, then you're probably a woman who is ready to build a successful business while living a life you truly love. Well, I'm thrilled that you've found this resource. I'm on a mission to equip Christian women in business with the encouragement, support and tools needed to follow their calling and be financially abundant.

My journey in business began when I became a life coach. I wanted to help women discover God's unique purpose for their lives. I was on staff at a church as a Children's Minister and seemed to be surrounded by many women who were just going through the motions of everyday life. I wanted to help them see there was more to life. So, after going through my coach training program, I decided to take the leap and begin a full time career as a life coach. This was a huge step of faith because I was single at the time, so there was no one to fall back on. I quickly discovered that though I had the tools to be a great coach, I greatly lacked the tools to be a savvy business owner. What on earth had I done? I had no experience running a business. I was a Children's Minister. And, at the time, I was only 25 years-old. Had I just misheard God's plan for my life?

As the fear set in, I ***decided*** that I wanted to be more than just a great coach. I also wanted to be a savvy business owner. Little did I know that it would take LOTS of work to master my craft (coaching) and become a savvy business woman. There wasn't a manual that I could just pick up and begin to utilize. I had to learn many of the things that I'm going to share with you through trial and error. Along the way, I made mistakes. And, I mean lots of mistakes. However, through those mistakes, I've discovered what works in business and what does not, which is why this book exists. I want to help you avoid that learning curve. I want this book to be the resource that equips YOU with the ability to build a business that allows you to follow your calling, make the money you desire, and live a life you absolutely love!

There are several ways to use this book. However, I would suggest that you start by reading through the entire book. Then, once you've done a complete read through, go back and begin working through each assignment. You'll notice that this book is intentionally set-up differently than most books. Rather than chapters, you'll see mini sections throughout the book. My intention is for this book to be a resource that you can easily refer to often. You will also notice coaching assignments throughout the book. These assignments are meant to help you immediately begin applying each concept to your business.

Scan this QR code using your smart phone or go to www.ibloom.co/business-book-resources for an online library of resources to accompany this book.

This book is designed to be the manual I wish I had discovered when I started my business. As your Business Mentor Coach, I want to help you drastically shorten your learning curve by teaching you a proven, step-by-step method for building your business. I want to help you be a savvy business owner as you follow God's calling for your life, make good money, and live a life YOU truly love!

Let's get started...

Life Essentials that are Vital to Your Business

Your business is only ONE piece of your life. Many entrepreneurs make the mistake of believing their business is their life. It's not! There is so much more to your life, than just your ministry or business. So, I want to begin this book with the life essentials that will allow you to **build your business around a life you love.**

#1

Reality Check

In order to begin building your business around a life you love, you must start with a reality check. This is your opportunity to take an honest look at every facet of your life and business. This reality check will give you a starting point as you begin to articulate your ideal life. Most of us would rather just skip ahead to dreaming about our ideal lives. Don't do that. Spend time here. Celebrate what is going well. Decide what you're willing to change. Since this is your one and only life, how do you want to live it?

Our core life areas typically include the following: physical health, relationship with God, finances, relationship with others, ME time, community service, personal growth, purpose, and our business or career. Carve out time this week to examine these different facets of your life: What is going well? What is not going well? What needs to change? Be very specific and honest with yourself as you describe the current reality of each life area.

Coaching Exercise:

Personal (Physical Health, Relationship with God, Finances, Relationship with Others, "Me Time", Community Service, Personal Growth, Purpose)	Business (Income, # of clients/parties, # of product sales, # of sales, Mailing List, Facebook Fans, Twitter Followers)
What is going well?	**What is going well?**
What is not going well?	**What is not going well?**
What needs to change?	**What needs to change?**

Having this honest snapshot of your current reality is the first step in moving from where you are to where you want to be. We'll discuss where you really want to be in Section #5.

#2

Why am I here?

It's plain and simple; we're here to honor God! As humans that's our universal mission. However, God has also equipped each of us with unique talents, gifts, strengths, passions, and experiences. You're uniquely different than me. You're different than your best friend or even your Mom. YOU are fearfully and wonderfully made. I love this passage from Psalm 139:13-17 (NIV):

> *For you created my inmost being; you knit me together in my mother's womb.*
>
> *I praise you because I am fearfully and wonderfully made; your works are wonderful, I know that full well.*
>
> *My frame was not hidden from you when I was made in the secret place, when I was woven together in the depths of the earth.*
>
> *Your eyes saw my unformed body; all the days ordained for me were written in your book before one of them came to be.*
>
> *How precious to me are your thoughts, God!*

God has uniquely created YOU just the way you are for a purpose. Have you ever really thought about that?

What is unique about you? Why are you here? Why has God created you the way you are?

It's through your uniqueness that you are best able to serve God and fulfill the unique purpose He has for your life. Once you realize why you're here, it will change the way you live your life. Instead of just going through the motions of this life, you'll have purpose and intention added to your days. So, start today identifying how you're unique.

Journaling:

What sets you apart from others? What is unique about you? What are your talents, gifts, strengths, passions, and experiences?

#3

Cultivate an Intimate Relationship with Christ

The most important aspect of my personal life is my relationship with Christ. For many years I subconsciously lived by what I call the "Good Christian Girl Checklist," it looks a little like this:

✓ Go to Church
✓ Read my Bible
✓ Journal
✓ Pray
✓ Tell a friend about Jesus
✓ Go to Bible Study
✓ Listen to Christian Music

However, I realized that God was far more concerned with my personal, daily relationship with Him than just checking things off a list. This truth revolutionized my life. God wanted all of me, just like He wants all of you. Are you willing to entrust every facet of your life to Him? As I said yes to God, I discovered that His plans were far more perfect than anything I could conjure up myself. He has your best interest in mind. He loves you unconditionally. And He wants to be in a personal relationship with you.

Don't get me wrong, I still do many of the things on the "Good Christian Girl Checklist," but now I do them because of my personal relationship with Christ, not because I feel obligated to do them.

The most important part of my day is my quiet time each morning. I think of it as the most important business meeting of my day. This is the time I've set aside to deepen my relationship with Christ. I spend time listening to worship music, praising Him, reading His Word, praying, listening, and just being still. Did you know that if you ask God to speak to you, He will? This was and is still mind boggling to me. The God of the universe wants to have a conversation with me! And, with YOU! God is so gracious and patient with us. He doesn't push His will or plan on us. He will wait until we ask and are ready to receive. The most sacred part of my morning is when I ask, "Lord, speak to me today…" And, then I just wait in silence. I'll eventually begin to hear that still, small voice. And, I'll journal everything I sense God speaking to me. I love the promise of Jeremiah 33:3, "Call to me and I will answer you and tell you great and unsearchable things you do not know."

For many years I was in the habit of barking my orders to God through what I called prayer requests. Each morning, I would pray, asking for healing, blessings, intercession, patience, perseverance, blah, blah, blah – then I would jump up to begin my day. It was pretty much the same requests morning after morning.

Just imagine a similar situation with a friend. You've both set aside 30 minutes to spend together. You're meeting for coffee to get advice about a problem you're having, but you spend the entire time explaining all the different angles of your problem. You glance at your watch and realize 30 minutes has already passed and your friend hasn't spoken a word. But, you're on to your next appointment.

How often does that describe your relationship with God? God wants to have a two-way conversation with YOU. It's not just us presenting our requests to Him, but it's also taking the time to listen as He leads. Here's a news flash: God already knows our problems. What if instead of telling God your problems, you spent time listening as He shares the solutions? I promise you this simple concept could revolutionize your life...it did mine.

You must choose to carve out time with God everyday. There is no task, activity, or meeting more important than sitting at the feet of Jesus each morning. This is your sacred time with God. He wants to speak to you. He wants to lead your life and every aspect of your business. Start praying bold, huge prayers. I mean prayers so big that they can't possibly be accomplished without God answering your requests.

What will you begin doing today to cultivate a more intimate relationship with Christ?

#4
Create a Personal Definition of Success

Do you have a personal definition of success? I remember learning about this concept for the first time when I was reading Andy Stanley's book "The Next Generation Leader: 5 Essentials for Those Who Will Shape the Future." In that book, Andy asks,

"Have you determined what you want to become? Your doing will flow from who are you. The outer man will reflect the inner man. The inner man determines the legacy of the outer man" (Stanley, 2003). I can remember reading and re-reading that statement (and the entire chapter) over and over.

As a leader, I knew the responsibility God had entrusted to me. I knew that people were watching me. I knew that I didn't want to disappoint or betray anyone. I knew that I didn't want to become like other leaders who fall, and fall hard. However, I had never really decided who I wanted to become or intentionally decided how I wanted to live my life, so this was the perfect opportunity.

So, I began to journal through questions like:

- Who do I want to become?

- What do I want to be remembered for?

- How do I want the people who knew me best to describe my life?

I created my personal definition of success by narrowing it down to ten words that I wanted to become: **Servant, Generous, Humble, Balanced, Authentic, Passionate, Relational, Loyal, Grateful,** and **Compassionate.** These simple words that hold so much meaning to me became the standard for how I want to live each day.

As Andy says, your personal definition of success "forms the moral perimeter around your behavior." He goes on to say, "You must come to grips with the fact that, ultimately, success is defined in terms of who you are and how you treat the people around you."

Coaching Exercise:

Who do you want to become?

_____

_____

_____

What do you want to be remembered for?

_____

_____

_____

How do you want the people who knew you best to describe you?

_____

_____

_____

What is your personal definition of success?

_____

_____

_____

#5
Creating My Ideal Life

In Section #1 of this book, I encouraged you to take a reality check of your life and business. I hope you've already done this, but if you haven't, take a moment to go back and explain the current reality of each of your life areas. It's really important that you have an honest and realistic look at where your life is currently before you begin to dream about your ideal life.

Did you know that you have a choice about how you live your life? You don't have to live your life based on the demand of others or in between each urgent need that arises. You can choose to create a life that is full of purpose and meaning.

Remember those Life Areas from Section #1? We're going to revisit them. But, instead of your current reality, you'll base your responses on your "ideal" reality for each area. Before you begin, take a moment to envision what your ideal life will look like.

Coaching Exercise:

What do you look like?

_____

_____

_____

_____

Where do you live?

_____

_____

_____

How do you spend your time?

_____

_____

_____

_____

Who is a part of your life?

_____

_____

_____

_____

What do you enjoy doing?

_____

_____

_____

_____

Once you have a vision for your ideal life- begin to think about each of your life areas. Use the coaching exercise to describe your "ideal" for each of the life areas.

Relationship with God:

Relationships:
        Spouse:

        Family:

        Friends:

Physical Health:

Finances:

"Me Time":

Business:
What do you want God to do in your business?

Now, compare your current reality, from Section #1, with your ideal life. What changes need to be made? How can you intentionally work toward your ideal life?

#6
My Brilliance Zone

God has uniquely gifted you with specific talents and gifts. In fact, there are things that you do absolutely brilliantly. However, the challenge when you are building a business is there are moments when you have to do everything – from the things you do brilliantly, to the things you do incompetently, and all the things in between. I know the feeling. In fact, when I first started iBloom, I spent hours and sometimes even days trying things that I had absolutely no idea how to do. I did research, studied, asked friends for advice, and then through old fashioned trial and error I would figure it out or give up. On those particular days, I was miserable. I felt like a failure because I simply didn't know what to do or how to move forward.

However, I loved the days when I got to do what I enjoyed. On those days, I would leave after a long day at the office feeling rejuvenated and energized. These were the tasks that I would have enjoyed doing even if I didn't get paid. These were the things I was born to do.

Do you know what I'm talking about? I'd imagine the same is true for you. That's why this exercise is so vital to your life and business. Unfortunately, when we're just starting our businesses, we feel like we need to learn and do everything ourselves. Sometimes this is because we don't have the resources to hire someone else or it may be because we feel like we need to know how to do everything. Well, simply said, you cannot do everything nor should you. Later on in the book (Section #24), you'll discover cost effective ways for outsourcing, but for now I want you to begin thinking about where you're brilliant and where you're not. In other words, I want you to identify the things that only you can do?

Coaching Exercise:

Incompetent: I have absolutely NO idea how to do *this* – just the thought of learning *it* makes me sick!	**Competent:** I know how to do *this*, but it is VERY draining & completely depletes my energy!
Excellent (acquired skill): I'm really good at *this*, but it is not fulfilling and doesn't bring me joy.	**Brilliant** (natural skill): *This* is where I THRIVE! I could do *this* all day long. I would do *this* even if I didn't get paid for it.

Once you've identified where you're brilliant, make it a goal to spend 80% of your time and energy working on those things. I know this may seem impossible, but it's not. Decide today that you're going to begin working toward this goal, one task at a time. Once you're spending the majority of your time and energy in your brilliance zone, you'll be amazed at how much more fulfilled you will feel.

#7

Managing Your 168 Hours Each Week

We each get 168 hours a week. Do you know how you are *really* spending your time? To help you identify how you are really spending your time, visit our online library for a coaching worksheet www.ibloom.co/business-book-resources that will help you track your time for the next 168 hours. To make the most of this coaching exercise, track everything you do in detail for the next week. This simple exercise will help you get an accurate picture of how you are really spending your time. Once you have the tasks, group your activities into broader categories. How much time do you spend - Marketing? Working with clients? With friends or family? Sleeping? Exercising? Doing personal care? Watching television?

The first time I did this exercise, I was shocked at the amount of time I wasted – especially watching television and looking through random photos of people I don't even know on

Facebook. We each have a limited amount of time each week, but it's our choice how we spend that time. So, are you spending your time on things you value or is your limited time being wasted by meaningless activities?

Download a second copy of the time tracking form, so you can create the ideal schedule. This will be a schedule based on your priorities and how you want to spend your time. It may be helpful to refer back to your Coaching Assignment from Section #5 where you defined your ideal life. Your ideal schedule should reflect your vision for your ideal life.

As a woman in business it is important that you also categorize your work activities. Possible work categories may include: marketing, writing, speaking, coaching, networking, administration, email, and planning. As you know, some activities are appointments with others, while other activities can be seen as negotiable time. Remember, when you don't have an appointment with someone else, you have an appointment with yourself. Don't allow others to steal the time you have set aside for important business activities like writing or marketing. These tasks are just as important as a meeting with a client or a networking appointment.

Once you've created your ideal schedule put it in your planner, so you can refer to it before scheduling an appointment or making a commitment. Be sure that your ideal schedule is a workable plan. If you find that you are rarely following the ideal plan, then it's time to create a new one that matches this particular season of your life. Your ideal schedule should be something you're constantly evaluating and adjusting until you have a plan that works for you.

Scan this QR code using your smart phone or go to www.ibloom.co/business-book-resources for an example of my ideal schedule.

#8

Making Time for Me!

As your Business Mentor Coach, I give you permission to put yourself toward the top of your To Do list. It's vital that you're taking time to rest and recharge often. As a business owner, you have LOTS of people and things demanding your attention. But, if you aren't taking care of yourself, then you can't possibly give to others. So, make a commitment today...right now...that you're going to take time to invest in yourself regularly.

Some possible "Me Time" activities could include taking an exercise class, having a girl's night, getting a pedicure, enjoying a hobby, taking a nap, going to a movie, or browsing through a local bookstore. "Me Time" activities are things that you enjoy doing just for you. Hopefully, your ideal schedule reflects brief moments of "Me Time" daily and more extended "Me Time" weekly.

Be sure to create a list of "Me Time" activities you enjoy, so that when you have those brief moments of "Me Time," you'll easily be able to choose something from the list, rather than wasting your limited time thinking of something you'd like to do.

Coaching Exercise:

What are your favorite "Me time" activities?

- _____
- _____
- _____
- _____
- _____
- _____

#9
Core Values

One of the most important decisions I made when starting iBloom was creating our company core values. I refer to these core values often because they are the compass by which we make major and minor decisions. I'm confident that God gave me these core values for iBloom. So, any time we are presented with a bright, shiny opportunity we funnel that opportunity through our core values. If the opportunity matches our values, then we'll investigate and continue to pray about whether to pursue it. If it doesn't match our values, then we immediately dismiss the opportunity. As a team, we review our core values at least twice a year to evaluate our progress and set improvement goals.

Our iBloom Core Values:

Balance- As an organization and team we model what it means to live a balanced, healthy, and thriving life. First, is our relationship with Christ and personal growth (physical, emotional, spiritual). Second, is our family and friends. Third, is iBloom.

Servant Leadership- We lead by serving and investing in others. We treat everyone-no matter his or her position in life-as we would want to be treated. We lead by inspiring others to reach their fullest potential, often beyond what they dreamed possible.

Integrity- iBloom is an organization of integrity. We strive to do what is right, regardless of the cost or sacrifice. In every decision, we follow the principle in Matthew 7:12 – "So in everything, do to others what you would have them do to you."

Enthusiasm- Our enthusiasm and joy for life is contagious. Our enthusiasm encourages a positive attitude and provides inspiration as we work together to achieve our goals.

Value Others- We help others recognize their value in Christ. Our goal is to make everyone we come in contact with "feel important."

Quality- iBloom provides premier customer service, products, services, and events. We strive to remain culturally relevant in our mission of inspiring women to live a life they love.

Teamwork- The iBloom staff is a team. We are a group of people who collaborate and interact to reach the common goal of iBloom being successful. We need one another to reach our fullest potential as individuals and as an organization.

Generosity – iBloom is committed to giving back to the community and to organizations that further our mission of inspiring women. We tithe 10% of our time and resources.

Coaching Exercise:

What are the core values for your business?

Value #1: _____

_____

_____

Value #2: _____

_____

_____

Value #3: _____

_____

_____

Value #4: _____

_____

_____

Value #5: _____

_____

_____

Value #6: _____

_____

_____

#10
Why Am I in Business?

My friend and mentor, Jennifer Thomas- Creator & Owner of Piggies & Paws, often says, "Your business is simply a vehicle to serve others."

When we are in business it can become very easy to focus on what we need from others. For instance, you need clients who will invest in your services- so in essence you need their financial investment. Or, maybe you want to do barter with someone, so you can benefit from their expertise in a particular area. But, what would happen if you shifted your primary focus from what you need (or want) to what you can give?

Don't get me wrong here. I'm not suggesting that you give your services away for free, because you shouldn't. I firmly believe that you have invested time and resources into developing your expertise and you should be compensated for it. Plus, when others make a financial investment in your services, they have a higher commitment level. But, shifting your primary focus from getting to giving will require a paradigm shift. Instead of being consumed with desperately needing people to invest in your services and products, you focus on how you can best serve each person who crosses your path. This means on Facebook and Twitter, at networking events, and even at the grocery store.

"In the same way, let your light shine before men, that they may see your good deeds and praise your Father in heaven."
Matthew 5:16

WHO, WHAT, HOW Principle

The WHO, WHAT, HOW Principle is the most important business concept to grasp in this book. Many business owners want to skip this step. In fact, I believe that most business owners who are struggling financially have skipped this vital step. So, please don't make the same mistake. The WHO, WHAT, HOW Principle is a concise, easy to follow method that will help you identify WHO you want to work with, WHAT is their biggest ache, and HOW you can uniquely solve their ache.

I've worked with many women in business who have gotten stuck on this step for years! They just could not decide, so they floundered. Please do not be one of them. You don't have to choose an audience or niche for a lifetime- just for this season. The WHO, WHAT, HOW Principle is your vital first step. In fact, until you get this step down, there is no need to move on to the other sections of this book.

The WHO, WHAT, HOW Principle will either make or break you as a woman in business. This Principle is what will allow YOU to be seen as the go-to expert in a specialty area. It's essential that you stay on this step until you have clearly mastered each phase of the Principle.

#11
WHO is Your Audience?

The first aspect of the Principle is to identify the group of people you want to work with. This was a hard concept for me to grasp when I first started my business because I wanted to work with anyone and everyone that had a need for the services I offered. Oh, and if they could pay, then that was always an added bonus. However, there are several problems with this thinking. First, the theory "If you build it, they will come" simply doesn't work. I often see women in business investing all of their time and resources into developing their craft – coaching, speaking, writing, crafting, etc. However, they are investing little to no time and resources into sharing their message and services with others (marketing). They just assume that because they have something great to offer, then people will automatically find them. That is simply not true. Daily positioning yourself as the go-to person to a very specific group of people is the only way your ideal customers will find you and the message they desperately need.

If you are like most women in business, then you have limited time and resources. Because of this, you must be very selective in where you invest these resources. You can't market to everyone. So, your WHO must be a group of people who are willing to invest in themselves and ultimately your services. If your WHO doesn't know they need what you have to offer, then you'll be spinning your wheels for years trying to educate them on why they need you.

Coaching Exercise:
What group of people are you most drawn to?

Who would you really enjoy working with?

_____

_____

Other Comments/Thoughts:

_____

_____

_____

_____

_____

_____

Once you've identified your very specific WHO, then it's time to discover WHAT is their biggest ache?

#12
WHAT is their Biggest Ache?

Now that you know WHO you want to work with, it's time to immerse yourself in this group of people. You want to discover...

- WHAT is it that is keeping them up at night?
- WHAT would dramatically transform their life?
- WHAT needs to change?

Your WHO probably has a lot of needs and aches. However, it is vital that you discover that HUGE ache that they are willing to invest time and money into resolving. In order to build a successful business, your WHO must already know they have this problem and it must be an interference in their life.

It's really important that you know without a doubt that this is their biggest ache. You don't want to spend time crafting your business around an ache unless you are confident that it is a real need and it applies to a large group of your WHO. I personally made this mistake several times. I made decisions based on my opinion or my own personal experiences, rather than cold hard facts. You need sound, concrete proof that this is the ache of your WHO. And it needs to be an ache many people in your WHO have, not just a few people.

So, your goal should be to immerse yourself in your WHO. There are several key ways to do this.

First, you must find your WHO. Begin brainstorming where you can find your WHO. For example, if your WHO is Christian Moms, research:

- Popular Christian Mom blogs
- Popular message boards for Christian Moms
- Churches – in specific groups (children's ministries, women's groups, etc.)
- Facebook Groups for Christian Moms
- Popular Twitter Moms or Lists on Twitter
- Internet Search of Christian Moms
- Your competition

Coaching Exercise:

It's your turn. Where can you find your WHO? Identify at least 10 specific places where you can find **lots** of people in your WHO.

1. _____

2. _____

3. _____

4. _____

5. _____

6. _____

7. _____

8. _____

9. _____

10. _____

Once you know where to find your WHO, it's time to immerse yourself in this group. Find out everything you can about your WHO. What popular topics are they discussing? What are they Tweeting/Facebooking about? What are their biggest challenges? Remember, your goal with this immersion is to gather concrete proof of your WHO's biggest ache.

Notes from your Immersion:

_____

_____

_____

_____

_____

_____

_____

_____

_____

_____

_____

_____

_____

_____

<u>Survey</u>

Once you've done some initial research, it's time to survey your WHO. There should be three parts to your survey questions. The first part should ask demographic questions that will help you easily identify whether or not someone is in your WHO. If someone takes your survey, but doesn't fit in your WHO, then eliminate them from your results.

The second part of your survey should ask niche specific questions. The purpose of this survey is to find the biggest ache of your WHO and are they willing to invest their time and money into resolving this ache. You'll ask questions like...

- What keeps you up at night?
- What are you currently doing to resolve your challenge?
- If you could receive support in one area of your life right now, what would it look like?
- If money wasn't an option, how could I best support you?

The third part of your survey will help you obtain more personal information about the people in your WHO. Because you'll want to go where they are, you might ask questions like...

- What 3 websites do you visit most frequently?
- What magazines do you read?
- How do you prefer to receive information (Facebook, Twitter, Pinterest, books, audio, in person, etc.)?

Once you have assembled the questions for your survey, you can create an online survey for your WHO to complete anonymously. A great resource to create a survey is SurveyMonkey (www.surveymonkey.com). After you create the survey in SurveyMonkey, you'll be given a link that will allow others to take your survey. You can then invite people in your WHO to take your survey. You'll want a large sampling of people in your WHO to take the survey – aim for at least 200 people.

Analyzing your Survey:

The next step is to analyze the results of your survey. You will want to look for common themes among those who took your survey.

What are the 3 BIGGEST aches of your WHO?

1. _____

2. _____

3. _____

What problems can you help your WHO solve?

_____

_____

_____

_____

What products/services does your WHO need?

• _____

• _____

• _____

• _____

• _____

What excites you most about working with this group?

_____

_____

#13

HOW will you solve their Biggest Ache?

Now that you know WHO you will serve and their biggest ache, it's time to craft your HOW – your unique solution to their problem! This is where you'll tailor your core message to your WHO and their WHAT. Do not rush this process. The way you answer the following questions will determine the direction of your business from here forward. Before you begin, ask God to show you how He has been intentionally preparing you to serve your WHO and their biggest ache.

Coaching Exercise:
Based on your knowledge, passions, past experiences, and training- what five unique solutions can you offer to your WHO's biggest ache?

1. _____

2. _____

3. _____

4. _____

5. _____

What is the ONE big takeaway that you can offer your WHO?

_____

_____

What keywords or phrases is your WHO searching for on the internet to resolve their biggest ache? (In other words, if someone needed to find you, the expert, what keywords would they need to use?)

_____

_____

_____

_____

_____

_____

What sets you apart from your competition (those offering similar services to the same WHO)?

_____

_____

_____

_____

#14
Create a Customer Profile

Now that you have a clear understanding of your WHO, WHAT and HOW, it is time to create a "snapshot" of your ideal customer. This profile will represent one individual person in your niche. To create your profile, answer questions like:

- Gender
- Age
- Name
- Profession
- Biggest Dreams/Desires
- Biggest Ache
- Imagine him/her lying in bed at night about to go to sleep...What is he/she thinking about? Worrying about? Dreading? Anticipating? Hoping for?
- Keywords that he/she is most likely to search for in order to solve his/her biggest problem
- Other Notes

Scan this QR code using your smart phone or go to www.ibloom.co/business-book-resources for a template to create your Ideal Customer Profile.

Once you complete your ideal customer profile, print several copies, so you can have them visible throughout your work space. My customer profile is in my planner and hanging above my desk. You will want to remind yourself of your ideal customer before doing anything in your business- before creating a product, before developing a talk, or even updating your status on Facebook or Twitter. It's vital that everything you're communicating from your business is specifically targeted to your ideal customer.

Become the Go-To Person

Now that you have a clear understanding of your ideal customer, it's time to position yourself as their go-to person. Think about it like this: if someone has an ache that you can solve, then you should be the FIRST person that comes to mind when they are looking for a solution to that problem. Throughout the rest of the book, you will discover a variety of ways to position yourself as the go-to person. Let's start by doing the ground work to help you lay the foundation for becoming the go-to person.

#15
Create a Service Funnel

What services will you offer your WHO? When I first started my business as a life coach, I followed the traditional coaching marketing model which was to immediately move prospects to clients. I've found that this model doesn't work. It doesn't work for coaches or most other types of businesses (unless you are a plumber or electrician).

We live in an era where your ideal customer wants to get to know you personally and professionally. Before your ideal customer will invest in your solution to their ache, they must know that you understand their problem and that they can trust you and the solutions you recommend. Building this relationship won't happen overnight – it takes time. In order to begin building this relationship, you must allow your ideal customers to benefit from your expertise in a variety of ways that are free or low cost. The best way to illustrate this concept is through the service (or marketing) funnel.

One important thing to remember is that this funnel is geared toward your ideal customers (or target market) – not everyone. It is vital that you keep your ideal customer profile accessible at all times, so you can continually remind yourself of the biggest ache of your ideal customer. Once you're aware of your ideal customer's ache, then you can begin building a foundation for becoming their go-to person. Everything that you plan and develop should be geared toward your ideal customer.

This sample funnel has 5 layers and yours should look similar, plus or minus a layer.

- **Client Leads**: You will notice that this is the widest part of your funnel. It is the entry point and you should have the most people in this area. Client Leads include a variety of different FREE opportunities including your: Freebie, Newsletter, Articles, Blog, and Social Media (Facebook, Twitter, Pinterest, YouTube, etc.). These free tools are your opportunity to position yourself as the go-to person to your ideal customers. Each of these free opportunities will be discussed in more detail in the "Marketing on a Shoestring Budget" section of this book.

- **Products:** The second layer to your funnel is low-cost products. This will be the first opportunity your ideal customer will have to invest financially in your expertise. Low-cost products are generally priced from $5-$97, depending on your audience and the type of product. Possible products are your ONE Book, Ebooks, CDs, MP3s, Seminars, Webinars, Teleseminars, etc. Later in this book, you'll discover some easy ways you can turn your service into information products.

- **Membership Program:** The third layer to your funnel is a membership program. Membership programs are a great way to package your expertise, so that you have residual, monthly income. Membership Programs are generally priced from $5-$100 monthly, but depending on your audience, it can actually be much more. Remember, the more access an ideal customer has to you and your expertise, the more you will want to charge. Possible membership programs are Coaching Clubs, Content Based Subscriptions, Mastermind Groups, and Inner Circles. Visit iBloom at www.ibloom.us for a variety of examples of different membership programs.

- **Signature System:** The fourth layer of your funnel is your Signature System. In addition to a Home Study Course, this could also include an in-person event, like a retreat or conference. Your price point will vary for this depending on the format of your system and your audience.

- **1-1:** The final layer to your funnel is 1-on-1 services. You'll notice this is the narrowest part of the funnel, so you should have the least amount of customers here and they should be paying your highest fees because they have the most access to you and your expertise.

Once an ideal customer enters your funnel as a Client Lead, you will provide opportunities to strategically move the person through your funnel – one step at a time. If this concept is new to you, then I suggest focusing on the basics. The must-have basics include an excellent Freebie (see Section #16), your ONE Talk (see section #17), your ONE Book (see Section #18), and a Signature System (see Section #20). Once you have the basics, then you can add additional products and membership programs from there. Remember, your goal is to move your ideal customer strategically through your funnel. As you create each resource, you'll want to be mindful of the next step you want your client to take, so you can strategically lead your ideal customer to it throughout your resource.

Scan this QR code using your smart phone or go to www.ibloom.co/business-book-resources for a template to create your Service Funnel.

I was recently working with one of my clients and she honestly shared, "I'm struggling with the service funnel idea because it sounds too much like a sales pitch for me. I just want to share my message and make a good income." Perhaps you're feeling the same way right about now. Well, just like I told my client, the service funnel is your way to serve your ideal customers. You've already discovered that your ideal customers have a big ache they are desperate to solve. So, your service funnel is simply your strategic plan for serving them well. From this point forward, any time you create a new product or service, you'll want to refer back to your ideal customer profile. As you look over the profile, you'll ask yourself, "What does my ideal customer need next?"

If you're introducing your ideal customer to new concepts, but then not teaching them step-by-step, how-to actually solve their biggest ache, then you are doing them a disservice.

Let's use my business as an example. For many of my clients, their biggest ache is working many, many hours to build a business, yet seeing little to no return for their investment. They have a life-changing message to share, but they don't know who their customer should be or how to find him or her. And, when they do occasionally find that perfect person, they don't know how to package their services, so their ideal customer can afford to work with them. This book is designed to be a ONE book, low-cost product that equips you (my ideal customer) to build a successful business while living a life you love. However, this book is just the starting point. I can't possibly teach you everything I know in these pages nor help you create a tailored plan for your business. This book is designed to teach you the iBloom in Business Model for Success and get you started!

In order to serve you well, I provide next step opportunities like our iBloom in Business Inner Circle. The iBloom in Business Inner Circle is a way I can partner with you in a very affordable way. In the Inner Circle I am able to invest in you and your business, as you implement each step that you're learning in this book. The Inner Circle includes weekly video teachings where we dive deeper into each of the concepts from this book, as well as a monthly Q&A session where you can get answers to your questions, receive accountability and encouragement, and celebrate your accomplishments. Plus, you have the added benefit of encouragement, support, and collaboration opportunities with like-minded women in business through our private Facebook group.

> Scan this QR code using your smart phone or go to www.ibloom.co/businessinnercircle to sign-up for the iBloom in Business Inner Circle. Your first month is my gift to you, so I can personally give you accountability and support as you implement all that you're learning. Just use the coupon code: **success** at checkout to receive your discount. This is a month-to-month coaching program, so you can cancel at any time.
>
>

Again, if I introduce you to our iBloom in Business Model for Success, but then don't provide you with an affordable opportunity to work more closely with me and the rest of our team, then I'm doing you a disservice. And, the same is true for your business. The Service Funnel is designed to help you create a strategic system, so you can serve your ideal customers well.

#16
Develop Your Freebie

The first resource that you should create is your Freebie. Your Freebie is simply a free resource that allows your ideal customers to get to know you and your unique solutions to their ache. Your Freebie is often the first step toward cultivating a relationship with your ideal customer, so even though it's free, it should be of very high value. It should be good enough that when someone receives it, they say, "Wow! I can't believe this was FREE!" The value of your Freebie communicates volumes to your ideal customer. If they receive a Freebie with high value, then they'll immediately know that when they invest further with you, that they'll continue to get more for their investment.

Here are 6 tips for developing a FABULOUS Freebie:

1. What is your topic? Your topic should be something that your WHO is desperate to solve. Your Freebie will address your answers from the WHO, WHAT, HOW Principle.

2. What format is best for your Freebie? Your Freebie should be downloadable, in one of a variety of formats including a special report, an autoresponder series, mp3/audio download, video series, or ebook. Choose the format that best suits you and your ideal customers. For instance, if you hate to write, then you wouldn't want to do a special report or ebook. But, if you love to be in front of the camera, then a video series might work best for you.

3. Develop great content. Your Freebie must share excellent content that communicates to your ideal customer that you are the go-to person on the given topic. You'll want to be personable, yet position yourself as the expert.

Milana Leshinsky (www.milana.com), offers this excellent list of "Top 10 Content Building Strategies," that should help you get started on creating your content.

- 10 things 90% of people don't know about _____
- 10 questions people usually ask about _____
- 10 mistakes people make in your area of expertise ___
- 10 tough lessons you learned while learning _____
- 10 reasons people fail at _____
- 10 things that drive you crazy about _____
- 10 things people need to know before _____
- 10 secrets nobody is telling _____ about _____
- 10 mental shifts people need to make to _____

4. The title of your Freebie should be catchy enough so that when your ideal customer sees it they immediately must have what you are offering. The title should address their ache and your unique solution to their ache. And, be sure that the title includes some of your keywords- you know those words people are searching for when they are trying to find you.

5. Remember, your Freebie should lead your ideal customer to the next step, which would typically be a low-cost product like your ONE Book. Be sure to keep this in mind as you develop your Freebie. What is the ONE next step you want your ideal customer to take?

6. Your Freebie is free, but you don't want to just give it away. Your Freebie is a primary way you will build a list

of ideal customers. Your ideal customer will receive your Freebie in exchange for their name and email address.

You will want to have an opt-in box very visible on your website/blog, so customers can opt-in to receive your Freebie. A typical opt-in box includes a place for the ideal customer's name and email address. In order to get an opt-in box, you'll need an email system that utilizes autoresponders. Once your ideal customer enters his/her name and email address, they will automatically receive an email including a link to your downloadable Freebie.

For a sample of fabulous Freebies and a current list of recommended email systems, scan this QR code using your smart phone or go to www.ibloom.co/business-book-resources.

Ideas for your Freebie:

_____

_____

_____

_____

_____

#17

Develop your ONE Talk

Interview with ONE Talk Expert, Betsy Ringer
http://ibloom.co/speaking
betsy@ibloom.us

Betsy Ringer is the Speaking Specialist for iBloom in Business. She teaches women in business and ministry how to develop their signature talk. Betsy also teaches on and provides products for The Personalities as well as other vital topics.

Betsy, what is a ONE Talk?

A ONE Talk is the message that you, as an expert, feel compelled to deliver. This message is your unique solution to your ideal customer's biggest ache. Then, once you have your ONE talk, you can easily tailor it to other audiences, but it's still your core message.

The big mistake many people make when they decide to speak is they think they have to develop many talks. The truth is they only need one. This ONE Talk becomes your signature message that people need to hear and act on. It connects people with your business or ministry and conveys the message of your heart with the people who need to hear it. It will become the talk that various groups hear about and invite you to deliver to their group or organization.

How does having a ONE Talk position me as the expert in my field?

God has given you this passion, this desire to help a certain group of people. You have experience and knowledge that can help others. You *are* the expert. When you learn how to put together a powerful talk and how to use it in different forms, you gain credibility and are looked upon as a professional. There is a song in the Sound of Music that says, "A bell is no bell 'til you ring it; A song is no song 'til you sing it; And love in your heart wasn't put there to stay; Love isn't love... 'Til you give it away." Your message is only a vision unless you deliver it!

Oliver Wendell Holmes said, "Many people die with their music still in them. Why is this so? Too often it is because they are always getting ready to live. Before they know it, time runs out." Don't let time run out on you. Get your message out. Don't let your inner critic or fear keep you from delivering your message. Step up and be the expert that God has called you to be and learn how to create and deliver your one powerful talk.

You must learn how to put together a talk that will move people to action and be courageous enough to share it in front of audiences. God has been working in you for years. You have been developing an interest, knowledge and passion that needs to be shared in a way that will connect people with you, help *them* move forward, and ultimately, make a difference in the condition of our world.

Why is a ONE Talk essential?

I thought I had to have a long list of developed talks for people to choose from. I thought the more I had the more desirable I would be as a speaker. Oh my! I learned so much about that. I had a long list of developed talks and then I would receive a request to develop a *new* talk that fit into the theme of an event. Over time, I learned that if you have ONE Talk on something that you are deeply passionate about and it is well crafted, then THAT'S the talk for which you will be known. Word will get out that you do a great job and you will get speaking requests for that talk. When you share passionately about the message you have to give, it will become clear how your talk fits into their theme or they will be motivated to change their theme!

When hosts for events are given lots of choices, they get confused and can't choose. They'll set your speaker's kit aside and go to the one that is clearer. Be sure to let organizations know about the positive effects of your talk so they can get excited about it for their group.

How would someone develop their ONE Talk?

Statistics show that speaking in front of a group is the #1 fear on the Top Ten Fears List – ahead of death, spiders and snakes, and confined places. Any fear of speaking can be overcome by being confident in the way your material is organized and by being well prepared. If you have something that you are passionate about, that you want to share, then you can overcome this fear.

You are in business to help others and share vital information. The key is to give people real tools they can apply but also leave them wanting more – so they will establish a business relationship with you. You are an expert and people are hungry to hear what you have to say; this is a natural fit with your business.

You want them to *hear* what you have to say. Your talk must be organized in such a way that they can follow you and that their next action is clear.

It is important that your ONE Talk stirs your audience to action. You want to establish a relationship with them so you can help them solve the problem in which you have expertise. You want them to take advantage of the opportunity to purchase your services, classes, or resources. As you begin to develop your talk, become clear about the group you serve. Who will benefit most from what you have to say? What is the one big point of the message you are delivering? Decide the main message you want your audience to take away with them. This one big point will unfold during your talk. Use an orderly process to deliver your message so your audience can follow you and be clear about the action you are asking them to take.

What are some of the key ingredients to a really good ONE Talk?

- Really connect with your audience so they will want to listen to you.

- Make sure you know your one big point. This is probably the most difficult thing to grasp. One of my clients had several wonderful points she was trying to convey, but as she delivered her talk, I could not determine her one big point. Once I helped her clarify her purpose, she adapted her subpoints and the important message she wanted to deliver became clear.

- Your main points must support your one big point. Three main points will allow your talk to unfold. People are familiar with information bites, but if we ask them to remember or do too much, we will lose them. Adult learning theory tells us that adults remember that which they can apply. I may think something is interesting, but if I can't figure out how to apply it, then it goes in one ear and out the other.

- Every point needs instruction and a story or example that will help client's apply what they are learning to their lives. All stories must be lively, succinct, and have an obvious application principle.

- Conclude by summarizing and giving your audience a clear next step to take. I heard a very well trained pastor give what he called the message of his life. He unfolded his talk, gave stories, kept us interested, and had great information. But when he was finished, he simply said, "If I could only give one message before I died, this is what it would be." Then he walked off the stage. We were all left with interesting information but we didn't know what to do with it. You *must* let your audience know what their next step is as a result of listening to you speak.

Betsy, for that person ready to create their ONE Talk, how should they get started?

Sometimes it is difficult to get started. There is so much swimming around in our brains and we know we have to put some order to our message to make it clear and uncluttered. I have been trained by two different speaking experts and I have been speaking for over 25 years. I've created a handbook that is extremely helpful for developing your ONE talk.

This step by step guide helps you become a speaker to make the vision of your business or service alive to others. With this resource you:

- Apply the BASICS speaking model to design your talk
- Determine your ONE BIG POINT
- Deliver your message with confidence and impact
- Move an audience to action

Also, sharpen your speaking skills with:

- Guidelines about effective visuals
- Collaborating with event coordinators to help them have a GREAT event AND have enough money to pay you
- Developing your style
- Turning your blog into a talk
- Turning your talk into a retreat

Get your questions answered about forms, marketing and creating products. This concise guide is your partner for engaging your audience and making a difference with your spoken words.

To purchase, *Create & Deliver Your One Powerful Talk Resource Guide: A Step-by-Step Guide for Entrepreneurs to Speak and Make a Difference*, scan this QR code using your smart phone or go to www.ibloom.co/speaking.

Remember, you have a message that people need to hear. You CAN become a speaker! As you speak to groups, your vision and expertise will come alive. They will get to know YOU and develop TRUST in you and grow their RELATIONSHIP with you, which will help your business thrive.

#18
Develop your ONE Book

Having a ONE book is one of the best tools for positioning you as the go-to person to your ideal customers. A ONE book is simply your unique solutions to your ideal customer's biggest ache in a tangible low-cost product. Through your ONE book, you'll have the opportunity to meet your ideal customers where they are and give them a vision of where they can be.

This book you're reading is a ONE book. I'm sharing with you my unique solutions for equipping you to build a successful business while living a life you love. For many people who read it, it's their first introduction to me and our iBloom in Business success model. The book is an opportunity for me to build a relationship with you (my ideal customer) and share my expertise on the topic of building a successful business. Throughout the book, I strategically take you from where you are to where you want to be by teaching you step-by-step strategies for building a successful business.

Having a ONE book is essential to your business. This simple resource will position you as the expert- credible, knowledgeable, and it is your opportunity to serve your ideal customer. Your ONE book is your way to build a relationship with your ideal customer, speak to his/her heart, and share your unique solutions to his/her biggest ache. And, because it is a low-cost and highly valuable resource, it is often the first financial investment an ideal customer will make with you.

Before you can start writing your ONE book, it's essential that you're very clear on WHO you're serving, WHAT is their biggest ache, and HOW you will uniquely help them solve the ache. If you're not clear on those things, then don't start this process just yet. It will be a better investment of your time to spend months working on clearly identifying your WHO, WHAT, and HOW, than to start writing your ONE book. However, once you're clear on that Principle, then writing your ONE book is a pretty easy process.

Writing your ONE book is much easier to do than you're probably thinking and with disciplined, scheduled time it can go from an idea to an actual book that you're holding in your hands in less than ten weeks. Just imagine, ten weeks from now, you could be holding your ONE book. How does that sound? Let me show you the step-by-step plan I used to write this book.

The first and most important step is to create your detailed outline and timeline. In fact, it took ten weeks from start-to-finish to complete the original version of this book and I spent three full weeks creating the outline and timeline. Yes, it's that important to your success. For each chapter of the book, you'll want to have 3-5 subchapters. Then, each subchapter will have 3-5 main points. It should look like this:

- Chapter 1:
    - Subchapter 1:
        - Point 1:
        - Point 2:
        - Point 3:
    - Subchapter 2:
        - Point 1:
        - Point 2:
        - Point 3:
    - Subchapter 3:
        - Point 1:
        - Point 2:
        - Point 3:

The topics for your chapters will be your unique solutions to your ideal customer's biggest ache. Then your subchapters are simply breaking down the solution into 3-5 tips or steps. Think of a subchapter like a blog entry. Each subchapter will be approximately 500-1000 words. So, your chapter will simply be comprised of 3-5 blog entries. Are you starting to see how easy this could be?

For the sake of this example, I'm assuming you want to be holding your ONE book in 10 weeks and that it will be 8 chapters plus an introduction and conclusion. So, here's what a sample timeline would look like:

Week 1. Create Timeline; Writing Goals, Outline

Week 2. Outline, Hire Graphic Designer for Book Cover

Week 3. Outline & Introduction

Week 4. Write 2 Chapters (or 1-2 blog entries per day)

Week 5. Write 2 Chapters (or 1-2 blog entries per day)

Week 6. Write 2 Chapters (or 1-2 blog entries per day)

Week 7. Catch-Up Week & Conclusion

Week 8. Edit & Proofread

Week 9. Format & Send to the Printer

Week 10. Edit Proof Copy

Once you have the outline for your ONE book, it is important to schedule "Book Project" time into your schedule. My goal was to spend two hours per day of uninterrupted time working on the book. Once you have the "Book Project" time marked off in your schedule, be sure to identify the specific task you'll be working on that day. For instance, each day in Week 4, your goal should be to write 1-2 Sub-Chapters (think the length of a blog entry). And, by uninterrupted time, I mean do everything you can to eliminate distractions – turn off your email; don't get on Facebook, Twitter, or Pinterest; silence your phone. This is dedicated time for you to work on your book.

For your ONE book, I recommend self-publishing. Traditional publishers are wonderful for other types of books. However, a ONE book is unique because it's a tool for your business that positions you as the go-to person for your ideal customers. If you went a traditional publishing route, it could literally take years to get your book published; whereas, with self-publishing, the process can take just weeks. And, since your ONE book is one of the best ways to position yourself as the go-to person to your ideal customers, you want it quickly.

#19
Create Information Products

Your ONE book is definitely a type of information product. However, there are others as well. Your information products are low-cost ways to serve your ideal clients by addressing your unique solutions to their biggest ache.

After your ONE book is published, then you should begin creating information products that expand upon your chapters (unique solutions). For instance, in this book, Betsy Ringer has a section about creating your ONE Talk. However, she's able to go into much more detail and actually walk you through the step-by-step process of creating your ONE talk in her downloadable book, Create & Deliver Your One Powerful

Talk Resource Guide. And, that is exactly what you will to do with your information products.

Information products can be in a variety of formats, here are a few:

- Book
- Ebook
- Workbook
- Special Report
- Handout (or a Series of Handouts)
- Audios (or an Audio Series) / MP3s / CDs
- Videos (or a Video Series)
- Teleseminar / Teleclass
- Webinar
- Conference / Event (in person or online)

You would be amazed at how many information products you could create, if you just recycled things you're already doing. For instance, any time you host a teleclass or webinar, immediately turn it into a downloadable information product. In fact, you won't even need to create a new sales page. Instead, you'll just update the wording from promoting it as live event to the download and then update your thank you page / autoresponder to include the audio download from the event. By updating your original sales page, you're taking advantage of marketing that you've already done for the event. So, now when people go to the page they won't see outdated information, but instead a way they can get the information product. It's a win-win for everyone.

Just like with a live event or service, you'll want to have a 6-8 week marketing strategy to intentionally promote each of your information products. You won't want to release several information products at one time and expect them to sell successfully. You must do a 6-8 week Launch for EACH product. You will learn more about creating your Launch in Section #32 of this book.

Don't get stuck if all the technical aspects are in your Incompetent or Competent zones. Techy things are very tedious and draining for me, so I get help! Amanda Taylor from our iBloom team refers to herself as our "Geek for Hire." These things are in her brilliance zone and she is happy to assist you with the details like editing your audio or video, setting up your payment button, creating your thank you pages and autoresponders, or any other technical need you might have.

Scan this QR code using your smart phone or go to www.ibloom.co/techhelp to discover how our iBloom in Business team can help you with your techy needs (web design, graphic design, social media, etc.).

#20

Develop your Signature System

Creating your own signature system is one of the easiest ways to turn your service into an information product. This method is simply taking the content that you would use with a client individually and turning it into your signature system. Once you have your system, there are several ways you can utilize it: with groups, as a home study course, or even continuing to use it with your one-on-one clients.

If you've already been working with clients individually, the easiest way to create a signature program will be to develop a 6-8 session group experience. I encourage my clients to schedule a start date for this group experience. Then begin their 6-8 week marketing and develop the program as they go. By scheduling the start date, you have immediately turned this from a someday project to a project that must be done by the start date because people have already signed up. You'll be amazed by how this simple strategy will put you into action quickly.

Before you get started, begin to brainstorm the 6-8 major topics and themes you typically cover while working one-on-one with a client. Next, create a handout for each session. Your handout should walk your ideal customer through your step-by-step process for addressing their biggest aches and your unique solutions. As you are creating your handout, keep in mind that you will want this resource to be applicable to your one-on-one clients, groups, and those studying at home. It is possible that your system could be an expanded version of your ONE book.

Once you have your handouts for each session, you will easily be able to combine the handouts into your very own Signature System Workbook. You may also choose to add other elements for different types of learners, like video or audio lessons.

Once you have your Signature System in a study-at-home format, you will be able to serve your ideal customers while you sleep because you've made your unique solutions available to your ideal customers at any time and at a much lower cost than working with you one-on-one.

Just like with any product, service, or event you will not be able to create your Signature System and expect people to immediately find it. You must now tell others and the best way to do this is through a Product Launch. We'll discuss Launches more in Section #32.

Surround Yourself with AMAZING People

It's vital to your business success that you surround yourself with amazing people who will support, encourage, challenge, and spur you toward accomplishing your goals. These amazing people should consist of like-minded entrepreneurs, mentor coaches, mastermind groups, virtual support teams, and your own personal board of advisors.

#21

Network with Christian Women in Business

Interview with Diane Cunningham, the President and Founder of the National Association of Christian Women Entrepreneurs
www.nacwe.org
diane@dianecunningham.com

Diane Cunningham is the Founder and President of the National Association of Christian Women Entrepreneurs. She helps women turn their dreams into businesses through her coaching, consulting, and mastermind groups. She is a "Business Therapist," author, speaker, marathon runner, and fun friend. Her mission in life is to inspire women to dream big, catch on fire, and change the world.

Diane, I know that you are passionate about helping women connect and collaborate as they build their businesses. Why do you see this as a vital component to being a successful entrepreneur?

This is a passion of mine because I can see the power of God at work when women connect and work together. We need each other because most of us had no idea what we were getting into when we started our business. As I like to say, "I had no business being in business when I got started". I had no knowledge of business concepts and no training in marketing. I see women in the corporate world being competitive and not supporting one another towards success. As a Christian in business, you have the unique opportunity to surround yourself with women of faith that you can learn from. And then you pass it on as you mentor others.

Without these vital connections, I would never be where I am today. In fact, one of the key people for me along my journey was Kelly Thorne Gore. We met in 2005 as we were both launching our businesses and we created a powerful team as we used each other for peer support and then began to work together in joint ventures. I consider Kelly to be one of my dearest friends and cannot imagine my life journey without her in it. And long before we had Facebook and other social media tools, Kelly and I created our own virtual team as we connected throughout the day by phone and email to discuss an idea, or get feedback on a logo.

What are 3 ways a Christian woman in business can build her encouraging support system?

The 3 ways that a Christian woman in business can build her support system boils down to learning to Ask, Seek, and Knock.

1. We have to be willing to ASK for the support we need from our current network of family, friends, and

connections. Often it is this close group that we love that can be so worried about us branching out on our own. We have to ASK for feedback and prayers. But we also have to be willing to ASK for the boundaries we need, which could be a home office or designated time for our business.

2. We then need to have the courage to SEEK outside training and support. This can be found in mentoring, courses, online support networks, live events, or free training calls. Invest in your learning and your personal continuing education units. Be willing to have time each week set aside as you seek to gain new skills. Allow yourself the freedom to learn from a wide variety of people and not assume that one person or training program will be able to provide for your every need.

3. And the final way is to KNOCK. This is when we have to be willing to step out in faith and offer our services. We have to learn to "knock" on doors both literally and figuratively. What I mean by this is that we have to be willing to take some risks by taking some actions. We have to knock on the door to offer our services by way of speaking at a local event, presenting at a networking group, or even just being willing to share our business cards with friends.

What benefits do organizations like NACWE provide members?

The primary benefit of an organization such as NACWE is the community connections and ongoing training. As women entrepreneurs, we have to stay up to date constantly on the rapid changes to social media and current marketing trends. Being part of a yearlong membership program provides ongoing learning, support, and tools. I love the support that NACWE members provide for each other in the private forum on everything from business ideas to prayers to resource suggestions.

What advice would you give to that Christian woman in business who feeling isolated and alone as she's building her business?

Use all of the free tools that are right in front of you with social media. Spend time each day connecting by both virtual methods and live methods. This might mean attending a women's networking luncheon or going to work at a local coffee shop for a few hours each week. I know that for me, both of these actions were critical in my building blocks as I launched my business a few years ago.

Final Thoughts:

Above all else, trust that God has a plan for you and for your business. Get busy doing what God has called you to do, not waiting on the sidelines for everything to line up perfectly for you to be ready. It will never be perfect. Start where you are with what you have. Be willing to fail. Yes, you will be failing a lot. You will also have many successes but you have to know that the failures will come too. The faster I fail, the sooner I know I will get to the next success. Allow God to show you the way. He knows much better than we do.

#22
Hire a Mentor Coach

Having a mentor coach is essential for staying motivated, encouraged, accountable, and moving forward. You need a coach who believes in you, sees your potential, and can challenge you to go further than you ever dreamed possible. You need someone investing in you that is further along in the business journey than you and who is willing to spur you forward. Your mentor coach should have a coach of her own and be regularly attending high level conferences and events that are helping her develop her skills as a coach and entrepreneur. There is great benefit to having a coach who is investing in herself because you get the added benefit of gleaning what she's discovering without investing those resources yourself.

Your mentor coach should be someone that you admire – personally and professionally. You should be able to see organization in the services she offers to her ideal customers. She should have a proven track record of working with clients who are financially successful.

You must hire this person. Do not try to exchange services or negotiate her rate. In fact, the fee of a mentor coach should be approximately two-to-three times your normal fee. Because your mentor coach is investing in her own high-level coaching and training, she will have a higher level of expertise than you. She should not just give this away, just like you should not give away your expertise. If you are serious about building a successful business, then it's essential that you have a mentor coach who is investing in you.

#23
Invest in a Mastermind Group

The concept of a Mastermind Group comes from Napoleon Hill's bestselling book, *Think and Grow Rich*. In the book, Hill describes a mastermind group as, "The coordination of knowledge and effort of two or more people, who work toward a definite purpose, in the spirit of harmony" (Hill, 1938). A mastermind group should consist of multiple people striving toward a common purpose. In your case, your ideal mastermind group would consist of like-minded Christian women who are striving to build successful businesses.

I personally believe that you should always invest financially to be a part of a mastermind group. By making a financial investment there will be a higher commitment level of members and the group should be led by someone you would consider a mentor coach. Refer back to Section #22 for the recommended qualifications of a mentor coach because the same qualifications should apply for a mentor coach leading a mastermind group.

There are numerous benefits for participating in a high level mastermind group, but here are a few significant ones:

- **Support, Encouragement, and Accountability**: Because your group will consist of like-minded women in business, you will be surrounded by lots of support and encouragement. This should be a group that knows your goals and will help spur you forward.

- **Differing Experiences and Perspectives:** Not everyone in the group will see things as you do, so you will have the opportunity to glean from each member's experiences and varied perspectives.

- **Resources:** Each person in your mastermind group will possess different talents and skills, as well as their own rolodex of resources.

When choosing a mastermind group, be sure that the content covered matches the current season of your business. For instance, if your business is well established and you have lots of products, then you probably wouldn't want to join a mastermind with newbies who are just beginning their business unless you want to completely revamp your business direction.

#24
Assemble Your Virtual Team

You simply cannot handle every aspect of your business. You need a team. Anytime I discuss this topic with women in business, I hear two common challenges: 1) I can't afford to hire help or 2) I don't even know what I would outsource. Can you relate to either of these statements? If so, this section is for you.

I personally had a big ah-ha about this very topic when my friend, Tammy Burke said, "We know that the CEO of Subway is not behind the counter making subs, and if he were, he would not be making any money." We laugh at the thought of this, but is this how you're running your business? Go back to Section #6 and look at your Brilliance Zone. Remember, your goal is to spend 80% of your time working on the tasks from your brilliance zone. For most women in business these are not only the tasks you love to do, but they are also the tasks that generate income for your business.

One of the most important roles I have within our organization at iBloom is being the visionary leader. That is not a role I can outsource to someone else and no one on our team is going to assume that role. So, it is up to me to spend time with God daily getting our vision, direction, and plans for the future.

What are the tasks or roles that only YOU can do?

- _____

- _____

- _____

- _____

- _____

What tasks or roles are causing you the most stress right now?

- _____

- _____

- _____

- _____

- _____

One area that I really wanted to personally outsource was housecleaning. Keeping my home a haven for my family is something I greatly value. And, for some reason I thought this meant I was the one who needed to keep it clean and tidy all the time. However, when I finally did the math, I realized that I could work for just one hour a month in my business and that would pay someone to clean my house twice a month. It was taking me much longer than one hour a month to keep my house clean, so hiring someone was obviously the best option. This decision is a win-win for everyone. Instead of devoting Saturday's to cleaning my house, I now get to enjoy and savor the quality time with my family. And, it's providing income for the couple who cleans our home.

Rather than utilizing just one person to handle multiple roles, I've found that it is much more effective to use a variety of people who specialize in their particular area. You might pay more per hour for the specialty person, but because this is their specialty, you'll actually paying less per project.

Look at your stressors from above and now the graphic below and identify the areas that you would love to delegate to someone else.

Task/Role to Delegate:	Priority:

One of my clients worked through this exercise and realized that an area she desperately needed to outsource was marketing. However, she felt like she couldn't afford to hire someone to assist her with this. So, I challenged her to do the following:

1. Create a job description for this role. Specifically define the tasks you want this person to do. How long are you currently spending doing the tasks on our list? If it is 2 hours per week, then start there as a goal for your virtual team member and increase the time or projects based on additional revenue coming in.

2. What would you have to do in your business to make the additional income to pay for your virtual team member's time? For instance, if you contract a virtual team member to help you with marketing for 2 hours a week (8 hours per month) and their fee is $10 per hour, then you would need to generate an additional $80 a month to pay them. What can you do to earn that additional income?

3. Ask God to help you be creative about finding the perfect person for your virtual team. Here are a few ideas to get you started:

   - Ask friends or colleagues who might be using someone for a similar project
   - Do you know any high school or college students that might be a good fit?
   - A stay-at-home mom who might want to earn a little extra income?
   - Check into resources like http://odesk.com or http://elance.com.

Any time you're tempted to do your business alone, remind yourself that the CEO at Subway isn't behind the counter making your sandwich. You won't be able to outsource everything from your non-brilliance zones all at once, but with a strategic plan you can delegate one task at a time.

#25
Assemble Your Personal Board of Advisors

I believe that we all need our own personal board of advisors. This is a group of people who believe in you and what you are doing. They would love to come alongside you and support you on the journey. I would suggest assembling a group of people with different skills and experiences who are at a higher level than you. Each person should be willing to pray weekly for you and your business, be a source of encouragement and accountability, and, of course, be someone you trust.

You might meet with your board of advisors individually or as a group. And, thanks to technology, your advisors can support you from anywhere in the world.

My Personal Board of Advisors consists of a variety of people with varied experiences, but they are each significant to my success. Because of the nature of my board, we have never met as a group. I meet with each of them individually, as particular needs arise. One of my advisors is a very successful business owner. His schedule is very busy as he runs several multi-million dollar companies; however, I'm grateful for every moment that I get to spend with him. He sees business differently than I do and he cares deeply about my success, so he is willing to ask me the hard questions and challenge me.

Each of my advisors guides me in a different area – whether personally or professionally. My advisors include prayer warriors, a networking guru, business consultants, and a financial advisor. These are people who are experts in their given areas and are willing to invest in my success. Your personal board of advisors should never take the place of your mentor coach or your mastermind group. Remember, these will be high level experts with busy schedules, so their level of involvement will look different than a mentor coach or mastermind group. If you are serious about building a successful business around a life you love, then you need a mentor coach, mastermind group, and personal board of advisors.

You have people in your life who believe in you and are willing to invest in your success. Start asking God to reveal who needs to be a part of your Personal Board of Advisors. Listen as He reveals each name. You might just be surprised who God wants to be on your team. Before you approach anyone, be sure to define the guidelines of your Personal Board of Advisors. How often would you like to meet? What will their role be? How can they best support you?

Coaching Exercise:

As God reveals potential people for your Personal Board of Advisors, jot their name down below:

Name:	Role:

Marketing on a Shoestring Budget

If you are like most of the women in business that I mentor, then you are probably petrified at the thought of marketing. Most of us genuinely just want to serve others. Selling our services doesn't come naturally for most of us. My hope is that as you read and begin implementing the resources from this section you will experience a paradigm shift. Marketing is simply an opportunity to serve your ideal customer by sharing your unique solution to their biggest ache. You have already done the homework. You know that your ideal customer has an overwhelming ache. And, you also know they need the solution YOU have to offer. **Marketing is simply your opportunity to let them know that you have what they need, which in turn will allow you to serve them.**

In Sections #26-#30, I'll share the foundational marketing tools that you must have to be successful in business in this technology era. Thankfully each of these tools are free or very low cost, so you will be able to get started with a shoestring budget. Then, in Section #31, I'll share some other marketing avenues that you might want to explore, after you are successfully utilizing the foundational tools.

There is one thing that you must decide before we move forward. Do you want to market yourself as an individual who provides a service or do you want to market a business name? There are pros and cons to both avenues. But, here are a few things to consider. It's much easier to market yourself as an individual who provides a particular service. However, you would not want to do this if you want your services to expand beyond what you personally offer. In other words, if you anticipate adding additional team members or if you want the company to continue without you one day, then you would want to market it as a business. Answering this question is vital to how you structure everything in this next section. So, spend some time here praying and dissecting the purpose of your business and assessing your long term goals. You may need some additional counsel. If so, please feel free to email me at kelly@ibloom.us and I'll help you identify which direction is best for you. Once you have a definite direction, then you are ready to move forward.

#26
Website/Blog

The most important marketing tool you can have is a website. Your website will serve as the first impression most of your ideal customers will have of you and your services. A website is worth investing your time, energy, and finances into making it a valuable tool that your ideal customers will want to visit and revisit often. Think of your website as your online store front. I'm sure you're thinking, "this sounds great, but how on earth do I do this and can it be done on a shoestring budget?" I promise it's possible! Most of the marketing tools that I'm going to teach you about are completely free. This one is not, but it can definitely be affordable and it will be worth your investment. You do not need to know the mechanics of how to create a website because a web designer will do this for you. But, you will want to invest your time and energy into deciding the content of your website.

Let's talk about the fundamentals of a really great website. You will want your website to be welcoming, friendly, and very easy to navigate. So, let's start with the basics.

What is the purpose of your website?

_____

_____

_____

When your ideal customer comes to your website, what do you want them to experience?

_____

_____

_____

How do you want them to feel?

_____

_____

_____

What next step do you want them to take?

_____

_____

_____

Once you have clear answers to these questions, then it's time to outline the structure of your website. Here are a few must-have components to your site:

- Your site should be on Wordpress. Your web designer will set this up for you, but Wordpress is a must! I could go into a long explanation here, but just trust me on this one- use Wordpress!

- You will want to use a customized theme for Wordpress- ideally 2 columns. Your web designer will do this for you.

- Work with your web designer to identify the look of your site. You'll definitely want something that is friendly and inviting for your ideal customer. Use colors and pictures that will appeal to your ideal customer. When they visit your site, you'll want them to feel at home. Use your logo on your website (and all other marketing materials).

- You need an opt-in box. A typical opt-in box includes a place for your ideal customer's name and email address. In order to get an opt-in box, you will need to use an email system that utilizes autoresponders.

For a current list of recommended email systems, scan this QR code using your smart phone or go to www.ibloom.co/business-book-resources.

The opt-in box will allow your ideal customer to request your Freebie. I know this seems like a big step when you could just give your Freebie away, but it's a vital step for building your mailing list.

Ideally this would be in the top right corner of your 2nd column and on every page of your site. Your web designer will do this for you. Are you beginning to notice a theme here? I hope so. Your web designer will be able to handle all of the logistics for you. You will just need to let them know the structure you want (just follow these bullet points) and then you'll be responsible for crafting the marketing language.

- In the 2nd column on every page (beneath the opt-in box), you will want links to your social networking sites (Facebook, Twitter, Pinterest, Google+, YouTube) and to your RSS Feed.

- On your navigation bar you will want to have the following pages: Home, About, Blog, Calendar (if you're doing time sensitive events), Services, Store, and Contact.

But, depending on the structure of your business, you may want to have additional pages too.

- o **Home:** The home page of your site often serves as the first impression. In the first column, you might want to include a note from yourself. Go to www.ibloom.us for an example of this. Other ideas for your home page include: links to recent blog entries, or upcoming events. As you're thinking about what to include on your home page, be sure to ask yourself, "What next step do I want my ideal customer to take?"

- o **About:** Your About page is your opportunity to connect with your ideal customer as you share your story and the purpose of your business. Allow your ideal customer to get to know you personally, your mission, and why you are passionate about serving them.

- o **Blog**: Your blog is where you will interact with your ideal customers on a daily basis. Your blog will simply be a place for you to post relevant content that will appeal to your ideal customer and their biggest ache. You will want to use catchy titles that intrigue your readers to read further. Your blog is the perfect opportunity to position yourself as the expert with a unique solution to your ideal customers' biggest ache. You'll be able to invite interaction by using open ended questions that encourage your ideal customer to comment on your post.

o **Calendar**: If you are offering events (in person or online), then be sure to include a calendar that allows your ideal customer to get more information and to register for a particular event. Your web designer can use a widget that will make this easy for you to easily update and maintain.

o **Services:** Depending on the structure of your business, you may or may not want to include this section. A typical service page would explain what services you offer. At iBloom, we do an adjusted version of this by offering our Get Started page. Go to http://ibloom.co/getstarted to view this page. On this page, we provide each possible next step for our ideal customer, rather than the typical outlining of our services. You'll also notice that this model fits with the service funnel because we provide several steps before encouraging an ideal customer to investigate our higher priced one-on-one service.

o **Store**: You may or may not be ready for this page yet. But, once you start creating your information products, then you will definitely want to have a one stop place where your ideal customer can view all of your products. For our example at iBloom, go to www.ibloom.co/store.

- o **Contact:** This is where you share your contact information with your ideal customer. Possible things to include: phone number, email address, mailing address (for safety reasons, NOT your home address). Your web designer can also add a form that will allow your ideal customer to request additional information, ask questions, etc. Once someone fills out the form, then their responses will automatically be emailed to you.

- One of the most important factors to remember about your website is that you always want to provide the immediate next step. So, as you write content for each of your web pages, think about your ideal customer and what next step you want them to take?

- Don't leave outdated information on your website. Always keep your website current with relevant content for your ideal customer.

- Do not feel pressured to create your website by yourself. This is something you will not need to learn! Remember your brilliance zone from Section #6? Your goal should be to spend 80% of your time in your brilliance zone, and for most of us, this does not include web design. At iBloom in Business, we have a team that provides affordable web design services that can help you implement each step we've discussed in this section.

Scan this QR code using your smart phone or go to www.ibloom.co/techhelp to discover how our iBloom in Business team can help you with your techy needs (web design, graphic design, social media, etc.).

At iBloom in Business we are committed to providing you with the most up-to-date resources, tools and ideas to help you build a successful business. Be sure to take advantage of the many opportunities available– events, products, and our blog http://ibloom.co.

#27

Writing Good Copy

Interview with Copywriting Specialist, Leigh Ann Napier
http://ibloom.co/copywriting
leighann@ibloom.us

Leigh Ann Napier gets to play with words as our iBloom in Business copywriting guru. She loves to take your mission, heart, and product information and word it in a way that your ideal customers really get what you do and then they choose to pay you for your service! Leigh Ann loves helping women in business earn a living doing what they love.

Leigh Ann, what is copywriting and why is it a vital business component?

Copywriting is writing so that your customers will take action, e.g. buy your book, hire you for a service, buy your product, share your message. Copywriting is vital to your business because no matter how amazing your product or service is, if you don't compel your ideal customer to take action and buy into it, it does them no good and you can't make a living doing what you love.

Why did you become a copywriter?

It really wasn't a conscious decision actually. I had tried many other things that never clicked...some I made a great income from but they were very draining, not fulfilling, and didn't fit with the needs of my family...others that I loved but couldn't earn an income doing. While I was on the journey, God revealed to me this talent I have with words that can really help people...and I get PAID to do it! SO, finally and thankfully, I have found my sweet spot.

I've always loved this quote and felt like I chased its content for a long, long time.

"The kind of work God usually calls you to is the kind of work that you need most to do and that the world most needs to have done...The place God calls you to is the place where your deep gladness and the world's deep hunger meet."
Frederick Buechner's definition of "vocation" in his little book *"Wishful Thinking"*

I would also add "your natural talent" to that quote. How wonderful that after searching for "it" myself, I now see that God was preparing me for this. Now, He is allowing me to take part in helping others meet the world's great hunger with their products and services every day! I help them share their heart in a creative and clear way that compels their audience take action.

Where would business owners use copy?

On your website, book cover, titles of products, subject lines of emails/blogs, in the content of their emails/ blogs... Copy is everywhere! It is everywhere you are trying to speak to your audience and prompt them to make a decision and it is directing them to the "one next step" that you want them to take. They may accept or reject your next step but either way, you want them to decide. There is power in taking action! If they accept your offer, great! If they reject it, that's great too because now you can offer their "seat" to someone else who really needs to be in it. Your ideal customers are out there...you just need to help them find you.

In Section #14, I challenged readers to create a profile of their ideal customer. How do you use this profile to write good copy that speaks to an ideal customer?

Oh Kelly, this is possibly THE most important thing to get right before writing copy. You want to know your ideal customer really well, chances are you may have even been her at one time and that drove you to do what you're doing now! You need to understand her ache, know what keeps her up at night, know what a day in her life looks like, what she struggles to get accomplished, why she may feel she is never enough.

Once you KNOW her, you can connect with her. Once you connect with her, you can offer her a solution to her ache. You can satisfy the hunger we talked about earlier. It is a beautiful thing when that happens! So many times I've seen God make that a win-win in business. The customer needs what you have and you need to know that what you are doing matters...well, that and being able to pay your electric bill.

What are the key ingredients for writing marketing language, so my ideal customers see my service as the solution to their biggest ache?

When you are promoting your product or service, start where they already feel the pain instead of trying to convince them they need something different. The best way to talk so your customers will listen is to take the time to understand their need. The best way I've heard it explained is, "When someone is buying a drill, they don't care about the drill. They just want the hole."

In other words, if you are a drill manufacturer, stop thinking you are in the business of making and selling drills. You may be making drills but you are selling HOLES! They are looking for a solution to their need. There may be many ways to meet that need. Will you be their choice of a solution? They will be more easily convinced if you are speaking their language.

When marketing a product or service, what elements should always be included?

Don't spend a lot of time and effort explaining why your "drill" is so much better than the others or about all of the bells, whistles, buttons, and gadgets your product has. Spend time talking about what they really need in their homes, businesses, families, lives- talk about the hole and how you are the one to fill it.

Think of all of the ways your product or service makes the "hole" they are after. Use those phrases, keywords, and feelings they would be using to describe their ache as they talk to their friends, post on Facebook, and tweet about it. The goal is for them to understand you really do "get" them and you are the one to help!

When a business owner or entrepreneur hires you to write copy for their website or particular product's sales page, how do you get started?

I basically do what I'm explaining that our readers should do... *twice.* I first get to know my client and the service/ product they are offering and then second, I get to know their client and their biggest ache. At that point, it's kind of like working a puzzle to see how they fit together, what words and emotions would drive their ideal customer to take action and start or continue a strong relationship with my client.

The goal is for my clients "food" to be what their ideal customer "eats". This brings up another point. They are going to eat something. They'll either eat junk food or they'll eat the nutritious good stuff that their "body" really needs that will help them in the long run. My belief when I am writing for my client is that *they* are the nutrient-packed, delicious meal that their customers are really hungry for. Not the junk food out there that may promise a quick fix or similar result but doesn't deliver. If they're going to eat something, then they need to eat what my clients have been cooking up!

What do you recommend for that business owner who really struggles to write her own marketing language and she really wants to work with you, but feels like she can't afford your services?

It's safe to say that if you are selling a product or service you need to sell those products or services in order to make a living. I know it is a struggle to invest in your business if you aren't making enough money to buy groceries but you've really got to start somewhere and then build from there. Without good copy, all your hard work just gets lost in the noise and you are wasting your time. You don't want to waste your time, especially the time you have in front of your ideal customer. So in order to move forward, you need to learn how to write good copy yourself or pay someone to do it for you. The latter is usually going to end up being cheaper and much less frustrating.

If you are struggling financially and need to sell your product or service so you can make a living doing what you love, then start where you can sell something today! What is your biggest potential for having a check in your hand by the end of the week or the end of this month? Is it selling books, offering your consulting services, selling a product that is ready to ship or better yet, ready to download? Decide what that one thing is that can immediately generate income for you and start from there. If it is a product, for example, you would want to hire a copywriter to work on that product's sales page. If it is an event, such as a teleclass or a workshop, then you would work on your event page first. These packages are affordable and will get you going. Then, you can work on the rest of your materials as you make more money.

It's easy to feel overwhelmed like it all needs to be done today. But remember, the goal is to get your customer to do "one next thing" so in reality, offering a lot of choices at this point would just confuse them and delay them from taking action anyway. Good news, right?!?

Scan this QR code using your smart phone or go to www.ibloom.co/copywriting to discover how our iBloom in Business team can help you with your copy needs.

#28
Email Marketing

Remember your Freebie and that opt-in box? Well, as your ideal customers have been downloading your Freebie, you have been building your mailing list. It's a win-win because your ideal customer has a FREE, yet very valuable resource, and you now have their name and email address for your mailing list. However, it is not enough to have them on your mailing list – you must now continue to build this relationship as you communicate with your ideal customers on a regular basis.

Have you heard of the 7-to-10 marketing rule? This marketing rule says your ideal customer will need to hear or see your message 7-to-10 times before they will take action. Your ideal customers will need to get to know you and trust you before they will invest in your services. And, one of the best ways to present your message is through email marketing. For the sake of this section, we're going to consider email marketing as a newsletter or Ezine. However, true email marketing can definitely encompass much more.

Keeping in mind the 7-to-10 marketing rule, how often would you like to communicate with your ideal customer? Your answer might be daily; as I'm sure you would love to have your ideal customers taking action quickly. But daily would definitely be too much. So, think in terms of weekly, bi-monthly, or monthly. What do you think is best for your ideal customer? What are you willing to commit to consistently providing them?

The success of your Ezine will depend on your content, and on your consistency to continue to build the relationship.

The purpose of your Ezine is NOT to sell. The purpose of your Ezine should be to build a relationship with your ideal customer, provide valuable content that addresses their biggest ache, position yourself as the expert by sharing your unique solutions to their ache, and keep them informed about what you are offering. Think of your Ezine as an opportunity to serve your ideal customer. Possible components to your Ezine might include a note from you, a featured article (that would also be featured on your blog), upcoming events, contests/giveaways, and links to connect with you on Facebook and Twitter. Your Ezine does not have to be elaborate, but it should be something that your ideal customer wants to read each time it arrives in his/her inbox. Not sure what they want to read? Ask them, regularly!

For an example of how iBloom utilizes a weekly Ezine, go to www.ibloom.co/getinspired to download our Freebie. Then, you'll start receiving our weekly Ezine.

#29
Facebook

Facebook is a great social networking site that will allow you to build relationships with your ideal customers. Again, building a relationship should be your primary focus for marketing on Facebook – NOT selling your product or services. The selling will come naturally as your ideal customer begins to see you as the go-to person for helping them resolve their biggest ache. However, even though you aren't selling, you will always want to keep your ideal customer informed with things like: invitations to upcoming events, products you are creating, client success stories, etc.

This section is written assuming you already have a Facebook account and that you are somewhat familiar with Facebook. If Facebook is completely new to you, then I'd suggest asking a friend or hiring a virtual assistant that is familiar with Facebook to help you set-up an account and get started.

I am often asked whether you should use your personal page or set-up a fan page to interact with their ideal customer. And the answer really depends on the structure of your business.

- **Are you marketing your products/services using your personal name?**
  If so, then I recommend using your personal page until you reach 2,000 friends. Once you reach 2,000 friends, set-up a fan page using your personal name and encourage your Facebook friends to find you on the fan page. You might even post something like, "Hi Friends! I don't use this personal profile anymore- please find me at [insert the url to your fan page]." Once you make the switch from your profile page to your fan page, then you'll only need to update your fan page. As you get new friend requests, simply send each person a quick email letting them know that you no longer use your profile page and be sure to link them to your fan page. Oh, and the reason for setting up the fan page is because Facebook only

allows you to have 5,000 friends on your personal profile, whereas fan pages can have unlimited likes.

- **Are you marketing your products/services using a business name?**

  If so, then I recommend setting up a fan page for your business immediately. You will then want to post the majority of your business content on your fan page and use your personal profile for personal updates to friends and family, as well as occasional business updates.

- **Important Note:**

  It is more difficult to manage a fan page with your business name than it is to manage a fan page that uses your personal name, especially since one of your marketing goals on Facebook is to position yourself as the expert to your ideal customers. There are times when it will be necessary to have a fan page with a business name. Our business page can be found at: www.facebook.com/ibloomwomen and my personal page at: www.facebook.com/kellythornegore. Though this set-up is necessary for our business, it is far more difficult to position myself as the go-to person. So decide carefully what is best for you and your business.

Facebook is the perfect place to have an ongoing conversation numerous times throughout the day with your ideal customers. You'll create conversation through a variety of means like:

- **Updating Your Status:**

  At iBloom, we follow a specific schedule for updating our status at certain times throughout the day. We use the scheduling software, HootSuite, that allows us to pre-schedule all of our status updates at the beginning of the week, or sometimes just for that particular day. I prefer to schedule all of my updates for the week on Monday mornings, so that it's not something I'm constantly thinking about each day. As long as you are consistent, do what works best for you.

  Here is a sample schedule that we use for iBloom:
  8AM – iBloom Verse of the Day
  10AM – Announcement (if applicable)
  Noon – Direct to Blog Entry (MWF) or Resource (TR)
  2PM – Question to Discuss or Fun Question
  4PM – iBloom Tip of the Day
  8PM – Quote (MWF) or Promo/Announcement (TR)

- **Commenting on Friends' Statuses:**

  Your interactions on Facebook should be a 2-way conversation. Do not be tempted to just pre-schedule your status updates and then never log-on to Facebook. Status updates are not enough. You are on Facebook to build relationships and this happens best by interacting with others by posting comments to their status updates and notes. Be sure that your comments provide value to the conversation.

- **Participate in Facebook Groups:**
  I see many women in business spending a lot of time in facebook groups with their like-minded women in business colleagues. This is a great tool for encouragement and support. However, you also want to make sure you're going where your ideal customers are spending time. There are lots of Facebook groups, so choose 2-3 groups where your ideal customers are actively involved. This will be your opportunity to interact with group members by posting valuable insight and feedback. Remember, you aren't trying to sell, but rather to serve your ideal customer by offering your unique solutions to their ache through conversation. As you do this, you will naturally be seen as the go-to person when they are ready to take the next step.

Other tips for utilizing Facebook:

- **Use a profile picture that represents YOU!**
  Your picture will speak volumes to your ideal customer, so use a professional photo that is a good representation of you as the go-to expert. If you are branding a business name, then you might want to also incorporate your logo with your picture.

- **Be authentic, but NOT negative!**

  Remember, your ideal customers will be watching you through your interactions on Facebook. And, of course, you will always want to represent your authentic self. Be personable, so your ideal customers can connect with you on a personal level. However, there is no need to be negative. Be mindful of what you post and how your ideal customer may view it, especially if they might only know part of a story. If you just had a fight with your ex-husband or maybe you are just in a really bad mood, don't share it with the world on Facebook – call your girlfriend or better yet, start praying!

  Decide ahead of time what you won't post. I recently stopped doing business with someone because they were continually posting negative things on their personal profile. My goal is to create an environment on my personal and business facebook page where people want to be. I want to be the positive, motivating, and encouraging voice they see on a daily basis. Decide today what type of environment you want to create.

- **Link Facebook & Twitter**:

  I highly recommend linking your Facebook and Twitter accounts. This will allow you to automatically update your Twitter status as you update your status on Facebook. A web designer or virtual assistant can do this for you. If you're using HootSuite to pre-schedule your posts, then this step isn't necessary because you can automatically post to all of your social media platforms at the same time.

- **Facebook Parties:**

   At iBloom we LOVE Facebook Parties. Facebook Parties are a great way to invest in your ideal customers and allow them to begin interacting with one another.

   The party takes place on your fan page and it consists of you (the host) asking a question and allowing partiers to answer the question by leaving a comment on your post. We mix it up with a variety of questions that might be serious, fun, or just interesting.

   If you want to host a Facebook Party, be sure to pre-write what you'll post during the party – the questions, promotions, etc. Then, you'll just have to copy and paste in your response throughout the party. We typically ask 10-15 questions per party.

   Though Facebook doesn't allow you to give prizes to winners anymore, you can still give gifts to everyone. So, this is a great opportunity to give everyone a free gift – your freebie! This is a win-win for everyone because your attendees are getting a fabulous gift that they'll devour later. And, you're getting their contact information, so you can continue to build the relationship and position yourself as the go-to person. Here's an example of what we post during a party:

It's Giveaway Time: We have a special gift for you! Go to http://ibloom.co/getinspired to download "10 Ways to Get Inspired!" by the iBloom team.

- **Events:**

  Anytime you are hosting an event (Facebook Party, Teleclass, Webinar, etc.), create an event page on Facebook. This will allow you to invite your ideal customers to attend, plus it is just one more way of positioning yourself as the expert with a unique solution to their ache.

- **Links to Facebook**:

  Include a link to your Facebook fan page on everything – website, email signature, Ezine, blog, articles, radio show, etc. Facebook is one of the primary places where you can build relationships with your ideal customers on a daily basis.

Facebook is constantly adding new or improved features that allow you to build a better relationship with your ideal customers. You will want to keep up-to-date with the different trends through our iBloom in Business Blog. Scan this QR code using your smart phone or go to www.ibloom.co/blog.

#30
Twitter

Very similar to Facebook, Twitter is a great social networking site that also allows you to build relationships with your ideal customers. The guidelines for Facebook and Twitter are very similar. Your primary focus with marketing on Twitter will be building a relationship with your ideal customers- NOT selling to them.

Again, you will want to decide if you are going to use your personal name or your business name when setting up your Twitter Account. Whatever you decided for Facebook is applicable for Twitter, too.

In Section #28, I encouraged you to link your Facebook and Twitter accounts, so if you have done that, it will make your interactions on Twitter much easier. Though your automatic updates will be done for you, this will not be enough to build a relationship. Your primary role will now be to interact with your ideal customers by replying to their tweets or retweeting their tweets.

Twitter is very unique because it often gives you direct access to many of the top people in your industry. There is no longer 6 degrees of separation between you and others around the world because Twitter makes it possible to instantly communicate with just about anyone.

Tips for getting Twitter Followers:

- **Create an Inviting Twitter Profile:**
  Twitter allows you to have a customized Twitter background. Be sure that your background represents your branding. I recommend using the same background as your website, so you carry through with the same theme. Just like with Facebook, you will also want to use a photo that represents you as the go-to expert.

- **Your 160 Character Bio:**
  Your one-line bio will often be your introduction to those who visit your Twitter page. Joel Comm, the author of Twitter Power, suggests doing a very simple format of "three, one-or-two word phrases that describe who you are or what you do, followed by a short joke to finish it off. (Comm, 2010)" If you want to create a bio like this, consider using his example:
  "[Professional description 1], [Professional description 2], [Professional description 3] who likes to [Personal description.]"

- **Make a list of high profile Tweeters who have the same (or very similar) ideal customers as you:**
  I would consider someone a high profile tweeter if he/she tweeted multiple times per day and had at least 1,000 followers. You can find high profile tweeters by searching Twitter for keywords, phrases, or by the names of

individuals or businesses. Once you have a list of 12-24 high profile Tweeters, follow each of them. You'll want to begin to build a relationship with these tweeters by interacting with them (replying to their tweets) or retweeting their tweets. If your ideal customers are the same, then start following the people who are following them.

- **Attend Twitter Parties:**
  Twitter Parties are a great way to connect with potential ideal customers. Do a google search of "twitter party calendar" to find Twitter Parties that would be a good fit for you.

Other tips for utilizing Twitter:

- **Hashtags:**
  The # symbol, or hashtag, is used to mark keywords or topics in a Tweet. To create a hashtag, simply put the # symbol before a relevant keyword within your tweet. A hashtag then allows people to easily search for relevant topics. You might also create your own hashtag to promote your brand or an upcoming event.

- **Create Lists:**
  One challenge with Twitter is that the more people you follow, the harder it is to stay connected with the people you really want to build a relationship with. However,

Twitter has a list feature that makes it very easy to manage your twitter feeds by grouping individuals together. A list will allow you to stay connected with the people you desire. We use the following private lists: Personal (this would be for your personal friendships), Power Players, Clients, Partnerships (or Joint Ventures), and Prospects. Once you have categorized specific followers into lists, then you are easily able to view the Twitter stream from each of the people in that group.

- **Host a Twitter Party:**
  Hosting your own Twitter Party is a great way to position yourself as the expert, while allowing you to interact with your ideal customers.

If Twitter is new to you, visit their Help Center at www.support.twitter.com to learn the basics of Twitter.

Just like Facebook, Twitter is constantly adding new or improved features that allow you to build a better relationship with your ideal customers. You will want to keep up-to-date with the different trends through our iBloom in Business Blog. Scan this QR code using your smart phone or go to www.ibloom.co/blog.

#31
Other Marketing Avenues to Explore

Thus far, we have touched on what I believe are the essentials for marketing your business on a shoestring budget- your website, email marketing, Facebook, and Twitter. There are numerous other marketing avenues that will help you build a relationship with your ideal customers. However, I highly recommend that you investigate these other marketing avenues after you are successfully utilizing the foundational avenues we have already covered.

Pinterest:
Pinterest is a visual pin board and it's a great way to connect with your ideal customers. If you choose to use Pinterest as a marketing tool for your business, you'll want to create boards that appeal to your ideal customers. www.pinterest.com

LinkedIn:
LinkedIn is another social networking platform that allows you to connect with colleagues (past and present), classmates and clients. LinkedIn is an excellent place to build relationships and position yourself as an expert in your particular area. www.linkedin.com

Google+:
Google+ is a great social media platform that utilizes the power of the google search engine. If you've posted relevant content

and keywords on your Google+ page, when your ideal customer searches on Google, your post or video may show up as options from their search. Google+ also has a great feature known as hangouts. Hangouts allow you to connect with up to 10 people via video at one time. www.plus.google.com

BlogTalkRadio:

Have you always dreamed of hosting your own radio show? If so, BlogTalkRadio is the perfect platform to host your very own internet radio show, simply by using your phone and a computer. BlogTalkRadio allows you to broadcast your unique solution to your ideal customers around the world. They even have several tools that make it very simple to broadcast live and past episodes directly on your website. www.blogtalkradio.com

Video Marketing:

Video marketing is a great way to allow your ideal customer to see you, while also hearing your unique solution to their biggest ache. Video allows an instant connection with your audience, especially for visual learners. Video marketing is a great way to catapult you as the expert in your field because as your ideal customers see high quality video content that addresses their biggest ache, then you will automatically be associated as their go-to person. There are many ways to utilize videos in your marketing including: coaching segment, promotional for a product or upcoming event, or sharing a tip of the week.

Article Marketing:

Article Marketing is another way to share your unique solution to your ideal customers' biggest ache. Article marketing is writing content rich material that your ideal customer wants to read and then submitting it to different search engines like www.ezinearticles.com. Before submitting an article, be sure to read the specific guidelines for that particular search engine. Fill your article with keywords your ideal customer is searching for, so your article will become a resource they will find when doing an internet search.

Press Release:

A Press Release is an announcement to the news media about something newsworthy. Press releases can be submitted to online search engines, radio stations, television stations, magazines, or newspapers. The news media does not necessarily want to promote you or your product, but they are constantly looking for newsworthy material. So, if you can pitch them a newsworthy story, then you are likely to be featured.

Joint Ventures:

Joint ventures (JVs) are a great way to network and collaborate with your colleagues, as well as more seasoned entrepreneurs. There are a variety of ways to set-up a JV partnership, including: co-hosting an event together, co-developing a product, list sharing, or promoting one another's resource. I have a lot of formal and informal JV partners whom I love working alongside.

To avoid any misunderstanding, I highly recommend that you work out all of the details of the partnership before you begin.

Networking Groups:

Participating in networking groups, whether online or in person, can be a great way to market your business. Be sure to go into any networking relationship with a focus of what you can give, rather than what you can get. Though you will definitely want to position yourself as the expert, your primary focus should be serving those God brings along your path. Do not join just any networking group. Find networking groups that are a good match for you and the customers you seek to serve.

Affiliates:

I am a huge advocate of affiliate programs- having an affiliate program of your own and being an affiliate for others. Having your own affiliate program is simply a way to say "thank you" for sharing my resources or services with others. At iBloom, we have an affiliate program that offers a 20% commission on referred sales for many of our services and downloadable products.

To learn more about iBloom's affiliate program, scan this QR code using your smart phone or go to www.ibloom.co/partner.

I am also an affiliate for others. I only affiliate with people and products that I believe in and personally use myself. Throughout this book, I have encouraged you to become the expert to a specific group of people – your ideal customers. When you do this, your products and services will no longer appeal to everyone. Being an affiliate for others not only allows you to bless your colleagues, but also provides individuals with the best resource for their particular need.

You may also choose to be an affiliate for products or services that could benefit your ideal customer. For instance, there are many resources that we use at iBloom that could benefit other women in business. These are resources that I am already recommending, so an occasional thank you check from the company is definitely an added benefit.

Guest Blogging:

Guest blogging is writing a blog that is posted on someone else's blog or having someone guest post on your blog. Guest blogging can be a great way to connect with the ideal customers who may not know about you or your services.

If you are interested in guest blogging for other blogs, be sure to identify blogs that serve like-minded customers but aren't necessarily in competition with you and your services. I suggest finding 2-3 high traffic blogs that could be a good fit for you and asking if you can guest blog for their site. If they agree, then they'll give you the guidelines for guest posting. Be sure that your blog post engages your ideal customer by providing high quality content that provides your unique solution to their biggest ache.

If you are interested in having guest bloggers for your blog, be sure to establish your guidelines before seeking out bloggers. Guest blogging can be a great way to increase traffic to your site, especially as guest bloggers will share with their audience that they are guest blogging for you.

Throughout this section, I have covered several marketing avenues that you can further explore. Before implementing additional marketing strategies, be sure that you are successfully utilizing the foundational avenues like your website, email marketing, facebook, and twitter. And, even as you begin to explore some of these other marketing avenues, be sure that you implement them into your marketing strategy one at a time. You'll want to wait to incorporate an additional avenue until after you master the previous one. The success of your marketing depends greatly on how consistent you are.

New marketing avenues are constantly emerging, so for up-to-date resources and tools that will help you best connect with your ideal customer, scan this QR code using your smart phone or go to www.ibloom.co/blog.

#32

Launches

Launches are a huge part of our marketing strategy at iBloom. A launch is our marketing strategy or plan for the promotion of a new product or upcoming event. Rather than having a set marketing plan for an entire year, we often have 3-4 event (or product) launches scheduled throughout the year. A typical launch consists of a 6-8 week marketing strategy that promotes just one upcoming event or product to be released. However, as a general rule, the higher priced the item, the longer you'll market. So, there are times when we have a 12 week marketing strategy. Yes, that is a full 3 months of marketing for just one product or service.

There are 2 significant phases to a launch- planning and execution. Both are essential to a successful launch. A well planned and executed launch will force you to be consistent with your marketing. The planning phase consists of the following:

- Identify the details of the project: What specifically are you promoting? What is the cost? What is your marketing language or description?
- Identify your Goals: How many tickets will you sell?
- Identify your Schedule: When is your event? How long will you market?
- Identify your time sensitive offers: Examples include: early bird specials or limited time bonuses.
- Identify your marketing avenues: What 4-5 marketing avenues will you use? Examples include: emails,

Facebook, Twitter, affiliates, blogs, articles, press releases (tv, radio, newspaper, etc.), videos, preview calls, joint ventures, etc.

After you answer each of the questions above, create a launch timeline. A launch timeline is putting all of your answers from the questions above into a systematic plan. Your launch timeline should include all of the specifics for how and when you will market.

Once your launch timeline is assembled, you will be ready for phase 2- the execution phase. The execution gets to the nitty gritty of actually implementing all that you have just planned. Begin by immediately transferring your dates and tasks from your launch timeline to your planner. Make a commitment to yourself that you're going to have immaculate self discipline as you implement each step of your launch.

I can't speak highly enough about having a launch marketing strategy. I personally believe launches have been a key ingredient to our success at iBloom.

Scan this QR code using your smart phone or go to www.ibloom.co/business-book-resources for a Launch Template.

Planning for Success

Throughout this book, you have learned the components needed to build a successful business. It's now time to bring each of the components together into your own personalized strategy for success. There is power in planning for success. In fact, planning is the key to moving you from where you are currently to where you desire to be.

Let's start with the end in mind. What is your dream for your business? One year from today, what will you be celebrating?

Today's Date: _____

_____

_____

_____

_____

_____

_____

I'm an avid planner because I believe that planning to key to my success as a business owner. Having the vision and knowing where I want to go is vital, but planning allows me to map out the steps necessary to make my vision a reality. Throughout this section I'll share my personal planning strategies. These are the strategies that I have adapted and honed over many years of planning for success, but feel free to customize them for your personality and style.

#33
Less is More

Several years ago I had a huge ah-ha during a retreat with my business coach. During her teaching she made the simple statement, "You should only complete 3 major projects per year." I sat there stunned. Just 3 projects per YEAR? How could that be? As she continued to teach, I pulled out my planner and began to look over my to-do lists from the previous week. I realized that even though it was only March, I had already completed what I would consider 5 major projects and there were many more already on my agenda for the remaining part of the year. No wonder I was feeling so exhausted.

During our lunch break, I pulled my coach aside and asked, "How on earth is it possible to complete only 3 major projects per year?" Before she answered the question, she inquired about my 5 previous projects by asking, "Were they successful?" And, then it hit me. I was doing a lot of major projects, but because of how many things I was trying to do, it was impossible to do any of them really well. So, with each major project I was either falling just short of my goal or nowhere near the mark I had set. No wonder I was constantly feeling discouraged. I was working so hard, but was really just spinning my wheels.

By trying to complete dozens of projects each year, I was leaving out vital steps that were necessary for making my goals a reality. For instance, I would spend weeks developing a new program, but then didn't market the program adequately because I had to be on to the next project. Then, I would sit back and wonder why my program wasn't selling the way I had hoped. Duh!

After that retreat, I started to make some major transformations in the way I structured my business. I made the choice to no longer chase after bright, shiny opportunities, but instead to have a strategic plan for successfully executing just 3-5 major projects per year. This simple change has dramatically transformed the way I do business. I no longer feel stressed or overwhelmed because I now have a realistic plan that has become my filter for every other opportunity. I typically work on just one project per quarter.

We'll explore this plan in more detail throughout the next section, but here's a visual of the method I use:

Vision/Dream

3-5 BIG Projects/Goals
(each project/goal includes a definition for success)

Detailed Action Plan
(includes 5-10 steps that will make each project/goal a reality)

#34
Annual, Monthly, and Weekly Planning

Successful planning must take place annually, monthly, weekly and even daily. Let me walk you through the process that I use year after year, because it works!

<u>Annual Planning</u>

Each year I spend several days away from my normal routine at A Quiet Place. A Quiet Place is truly my favorite place on earth. It's a beautiful retreat center secluded from the normal pace of life – there is no phone, internet, or cable TV. Thankfully it does have many other luxuries like Temper-pedic beds, cozy blankets, yummy food, jacuzzi, fireplace, walking trails, and a wraparound porch with lots of outdoor seating- including my favorite swing. During this time away, you'd find me...

- Sleeping: I tend to sleep a lot during this time away. I sleep later, take long naps, and even go to bed very early most nights.

- Cultivating my Relationship with God: I spend a lot of time studying scripture, praying, journaling, practicing silence and solitude, and then listening for God's still, small voice.

- Reading: I usually take a couple of books that I've wanted to read, but just haven't had the chance.

- Enjoying Me Time: I often partake in fun, girly movies, a bubble bath, a long walk on the trail, sometimes even a manicure and pedicure.

- Reflecting & Celebrating: I take time to reflect, evaluate, and celebrate all that has happened over the past year. How have I personally grown? What has God done? Did the vision become reality? How can I continue to improve? Where did we succeed? What can we adjust for the upcoming year?

After spending a couple of days resting and getting rejuvenated, I then start my annual planning process. Annual planning is a time set apart to seek God, His vision, and plan for the upcoming year. During this time away, I identify each of the items in the diagram below.

Before I begin, I gather a few supplies...

- Journal – this is always a new journal devoted exclusively to my business for the next 12 months.

It's a place to journal my vision, projects/goals, action plan, praises, prayers, ah-ha's, etc.

- Mini Post-It Notes (I LOVE Post-It Notes!)
- Pen, Markers, and Highlighters

I personally like to journal my prayers, so I start this process by writing something like, "Lord, what is your vision and direction for the upcoming year?"

I sit and wait, listening for God's still, small voice. As ideas and thoughts come to mind, I journal anything that I sense God speaking to me. Now, don't get me wrong, God doesn't speak to me audibly. But, I do sense things in my Spirit that I believe are little nudges from Him. This process can take hours or sometimes days. Do not rush the process. This is your time to connect with God and get His direction for where He wants to lead your business. I personally can't think of a better business partner.

Once I feel like I have a clear vision, then it's time to move on to identifying my 3-5 BIG projects for the upcoming year. My 3-5 BIG projects are always the big steps that will make the vision a reality. BIG projects are typically large enough that they generally require 5-10 steps to accomplish the goal. As you are thinking about your 3-5 BIG projects, you should have a variety of ideas just from reading this book, including developing your signature system, implementing a marketing strategy, writing your ONE book, etc.

After I've identified my 3-5 BIG projects, then I define what success will look like for each of these projects by creating a SMART goal (or definition of success) for each project.

SMART Goal:

Specific: What will I accomplish?
Measurable: What is the criteria for measuring progress?
Attainable: How can the goal be accomplished?
Relevant: Do I really believe this can be accomplished?
Time-bound: When will it be accomplished?

Once I know my 3-5 BIG projects and have identified each projects' definition for success, it's time to determine what 5-10 action steps will make each project a reality. I typically write each of the steps on a mini post-it note, so that I'm easily able to prioritize the steps in my journal later.

Let me give you a real-life example:

BIG Project: Write my ONE Book for iBloom in Business.

SMART GOAL: I will write & publish my ONE Book for iBloom in Business by March 2013.

5-10 Action Steps:
1. Survey my WHO
2. Create the Book Outline
3. Create a Writing Schedule & Timeline
4. Write the Manuscript (obviously this is a HUGE step that had to be broken down into LOTS of smaller steps)
5. Get an AMAZING Editor

6. Find a FABULOUS Graphic Designer to design the cover

7. Finalize the publishing details with iBloom Publishing

8. Develop web resources to accompany the book

9. Develop & Execute the marketing strategy for promoting the book (this is also a HUGE step that had to be broken down into lots of smaller steps)

I follow this same strategy for each of my BIG projects, so that by the end of my annual planning week, I typically have a concise strategic plan for how I will accomplish each project. Once I have the steps, then it's time to create a timeline for when I'll accomplish each action step throughout the upcoming year.

Scan this QR code using your smart phone or go to www.ibloom.co/business-book-resources to download your annual planning tools.

Before I finish my annual planning, I schedule one full day each month for solitude and monthly planning.

If you don't feel ready to walk through this process of annual planning by yourself, then you might find it beneficial to go through it with me as your mentor coach. Each year, I facilitate these personal retreat experiences with women in business who are ready to take their business to the next level. If you're interested in learning more, please email me at kelly@ibloom.us.

Monthly Planning

Monthly planning is equally as important as the annual planning because it's a full day set aside each month to get refocused and reenergized. I incorporate my monthly planning as part of my solitude days. During this time of solitude and monthly planning, I spend the morning cultivating my relationship with God by reading scripture, praying, and journaling. Then, I spend the afternoon reviewing my 12-month at-a glance calendar and creating my detailed plan for the upcoming month.

I am a very visual learner, so it works best for me to use a paper system for my calendar and to-do lists. For several years now, I have used the PlannerPad system and still LOVE it! Go to www.plannerpads.com for more information. This is the system that works best for me, but you'll want to determine what works best for you. You can use virtually any system that will allow you to schedule appointments and manage a detailed to-do list.

In addition to your project planning, you will also have other things that need to be incorporated into your schedule like client appointments, networking meetings, mastermind meetings, appointments with your mentor coach, social media updates, etc. For this type of planning, I have an "ideal schedule." My ideal schedule allows me to make time for what is most important, rather than wondering how my calendar got full, but I don't have time to work on my projects. The ideal schedule is a template that I use to funnel all possible appointments and meetings. On my ideal schedule, I set aside blocks of time each day for specific things like:

- Quiet Time (Bible Study, Prayer & Journaling)
- Meeting with my Mentor Coach
- Client Appointments – this allows me to control my time, rather than my clients! I no longer feel guilty about having a waiting list or having to schedule a client appointment for 3 weeks from when they requested it.
- Marketing – this is when I schedule my social media updates, writing blog entries and articles, etc.
- Project – this is when I work on the actions steps of my BIG projects. Depending on the project, this may be whole days or just a few hours a couple of days a week. Often times your projects are opportunities to work on your business, so this project time is vital for future business growth.

The ideal schedule allows me to dictate how I spend my time, rather than allowing others to control my schedule. This method is what allows me to work on my BIG projects. The ideal schedule allows me time for what I know is most important, rather than constantly changing my schedule for what seems most urgent at that moment.

Scan this QR code using your smart phone or go to
www.ibloom.co/business-book-resources for an example of
my ideal schedule and to download a template for creating
your own.

At the end of my solitude and monthly planning day, I know what BIG project I'm working on and what action steps need to be accomplished to get me closer to my goal. And, I've scheduled each of the action steps into the designated week that I'll work on them. In essence, I have a detailed plan for the upcoming month.

Weekly Planning

I like to do my weekly planning for the upcoming week on Friday or Sunday afternoons because this allows me to begin Monday morning knowing exactly what needs to be accomplished. Weekly planning doesn't take long because you already have your ideal schedule and your annual and monthly plans. Weekly planning is taking the work you have already done and planning what you will do each day of the upcoming week. You can ask yourself questions like:

- What tasks need to be completed?
- Who do I need to follow-up with?
- What appointments need to be scheduled?

The PlannerPad System makes weekly planning very easy because it separates your appointments from your daily to-do list. You can easily plug each of your tasks for the designated day into the daily to-do list without taking up space in the appointments area of your calendar.

Just one other important note about annual, monthly, and weekly planning: BE FLEXIBLE! If you follow this method, then you'll have a detailed plan, but life will still happen. Things won't always go according to your plan. And, that is ok. The beauty of having a plan is that once you have the plan, you can easily adapt it for when life does happen.

For instance, when I wrote Empowering Coaches (the first version of this book), I had planned to complete it 6 months earlier, but life happened. Shortly into the writing process, it was very obvious that my Dad was in his final days after a heroic battle with cancer. So, I took a hiatus from the project to care for my Dad. The book got out later than I planned, but that was ok. I lived into my priorities and because of that I was able to share so many precious memories with my Dad during his final days. And, since I already had the plan, once I was able to pick up this project again, it was easy to adjust the timeline and get back to work.

Of course you should be flexible, but don't use flexibility as an excuse to not work hard toward your goals. There will always be bright, shiny opportunities seeking to distract you from your plan. Be sure that any time you intentionally choose to put a project on hold that it's because you know without a doubt that is how God is leading you. If you are spending time with Him each day, then He will show you exactly how to invest your time and energy.

#35
Income Goal

I recently met with a client who is a newbie to business. She had finished her specialty training a few months prior, but didn't have a website or any products. Yet her income goal was to make $100,000 in her first year. This didn't seem like a realistic goal for her, but I was curious as to her plan for making this goal a reality. As I probed deeper, I discovered that she had really just pulled a number out of thin air.

In this section, I want to help you identify a realistic income goal and also help you create a plan for making your income goal a reality. As I'm sure you have seen throughout this book, I'm not an advocate for trading time for money. I believe that you should have multiple revenue streams from avenues like your ONE book, ONE Talk, information products, membership programs, etc. However, I do think it's really important to get a clear understanding of how much your time is worth. By knowing what each hour is worth, you'll easily be able to quote project fees, know when to outsource particular projects, and you'll be amazed at how motivated you become each hour you're working. So, here's an example from a client whose income goal is $50,000:

> **Annual Income Goal**: $50,000
>
> **Working Weeks:** 46 weeks (6 weeks of vacation)
> **Days per Week:** Working 4 days per week
> **Hours per Day:** Working 7.5 hours per day – 30 hours per week
>
> **Monthly Rate: $4,167**
> **Weekly Rate: $1,087**
> **Daily Rate: $271.75**
> **Hourly Rate: $36**

One of the great advantages of being self-employed is that we get to set our own schedule. However, this can also be a great challenge, especially when your family and friends might not understand that you are working. So, even though I'm not suggesting that you trade your time for money, I do think it's important to know how much money you need to make each hour or day to meet your financial goals. Trust me, knowing this information will be very beneficial when your girlfriends want you to play hooky on a work day.

Based on this example, you would need to make $1,087 a week and, of course, there are a variety of ways to do this: speaking engagements, product sales, mastermind groups, one-on-one appointments, etc. For example, if you had a speaking engagement that made $750 and you sold 100 copies of your ONE book for a profit of $7 per book, then you would have exceeded your weekly goal through just one speaking engagement. Knowing how much money you need to make each hour, day, and week will help you to know how closely on target you are to reaching your goal.

In order to set a realistic income goal, you will need to do a revenue projection, so you will want to ask yourself questions like:

- What are my different types of revenue streams?
- What are my price points for each revenue stream?
- How many do I need to sell for each revenue stream?

Here's an example with just one type of revenue stream:

- **Service:** 4-week Webinar Series
- **Price Point:** $50 per person
- **# of people in the Webinar:** 20
- **Monthly Income -** $1,000 for the Webinar Series

You will want to follow the same method for each of your revenue streams, so that you can identify what might be a realistic income goal for you. In other words, if you have a goal of making $50,000 per year from your business, then you'll want to make sure that your revenue projections reflect that income goal. If they don't, then you have several options. You could raise your price-per-person, offer more opportunities, or create and sell additional information products.

Coaching Assignment:

Annual Income Goal: $_____

Working Weeks: ____ weeks (__ wks of vacation)

Days per Week: Working ____ days per week

Hours per Day: Working ____ hours per day

____ hours per week

Monthly Rate: $_____

Weekly Rate: $_____

Daily Rate: $_____

Hourly Rate: $_____

If you would like assistance in identifying your income goal and revenue projections, then I would be happy to assist you. Please email me at kelly@ibloom.us.

Conclusion

This book has been such a labor of love. It's the book that I wish I had read when I started my business. I've seen so many people go into business only to become discouraged when they struggle to make ends meet month after month. I can relate because that also described my journey for several years. I would work so hard, but see such little fruit for my labor. But, it was during those hard years that I learned many of the lessons that I've just shared with you. I realize now that God had to take me through those difficult years, so He could show me the formula that works and so I could help you avoid the learning curve.

In closing, I want to leave you with six big takeaways from this book. In other words, if you haven't gotten anything else out of this book, then I want you to have these words and lessons to refer back to often.

Lesson #1:
God wants to be a partner in your business! It is your responsibility to meet with Him each morning to get your direction and vision for that day. Cultivate an intimate relationship with Him by reading His word, memorizing scripture, praying, journaling, and listening for His still, small voice. Don't even think about beginning your workday without that sacred time with Him each morning.

Lesson #2:
Live into your priorities. It's vital that you know your top 5 priorities and that you're living into them on a daily basis. When

you're building a business, you'll be tempted to put the rest of your life on hold for the sake of the business. Don't do it! I promise you that your business is not more important than your relationship with God, your spouse (if you're married), your kids (if you have them), your family, or your friends. This life is not a dress rehearsal. This is your one and only life, and though your business is a piece of your life, it is not your entire life. So, be sure that you know your priorities and that your schedule reflects that you are valuing those things that are most important to you.

Lesson #3:

Work toward your long-term vision that is broken down into short-term goals or tasks. Don't get absorbed in short-term tasks that aren't attached to a long-term vision. Don't chase after bright, shiny opportunities. Refer back to the Planning for Success section often. Building a successful business will not happen overnight or even within a few months. It will take time to create and implement the pieces to the formula you have learned in this book. Don't rush the process. It's vital that you know your long-term vision, have your 3-5 BIG projects/goals, and then work on your 5-10 steps that will make each of your projects/goals a reality.

Lesson #4:

Don't compete with others! Don't be jealous when others get recognition or seem to be more successful than you are at the moment. You are the go-to person to your WHO, which means there are plenty of other people serving a different WHO that you will be able to partner, network, and collaborate with along the way. If you have even a hint of jealousy, confess it to God immediately and allow Him to transform your jealousy into genuine celebration for that person.

Lesson #5:

I love this wise statement from my dear friend and mentor, Jennifer Thomas- Creator and Owner of Piggies & Paws: "Your business is simply a vehicle to serve others." Don't be focused on what you can get from others (especially money), but instead focus on how you can serve those God brings along your path. This doesn't mean that you give your services away – because you shouldn't! But, it does mean that you shift your focus from desperately wanting someone to invest in your services to focusing on how you can best serve them.

Lesson #6:

Invest in your own personal business growth by hiring a mentor coach and investing in a paid mastermind group. Investing in your personal business growth is the BEST money you can spend on your business. Don't be tempted to go at this alone. If you do, then it will take you much, much longer to build a successful business. For many years, I naively thought that I couldn't afford a business mentor. So I just participated in multiple free teleclasses, signed-up for free Ezines, and invested in books that could teach me what I needed to know – then all I had to do was bring it all together for what applied to my business. That was such a mistake. I now realize that I can't afford not to have a mentor coach and a mastermind group. Both are necessities to my business success and yours.

Throughout this book, you have discovered the pieces necessary for building a successful business. Your next step is to begin implementing all that you've learned and I would love the opportunity to support you and your business as you do so. Our iBloom in Business Inner Circle is one of the best ways that I can personally partner with you and your business as you implement each step from this success model.

Scan this QR code using your smart phone or go to www.ibloom.co/businessinnercircle to sign-up for the iBloom in Business Inner Circle. Your first month is my gift to you, so I can personally give you accountability and support as you implement all that you've learned. Just use the coupon code: **success** at checkout to receive your discount. This is a month-to-month coaching program, so you can cancel at any time.

My prayer is that you now have the resources that will equip YOU to build a business that allows you to follow your calling, make the money you desire, and live a life you absolutely love! There are many people who need the message God has given you. Ask God for His vision for your business, and follow Him with perseverance and tenacity as you make His vision a reality. You can do this!

References

Comm, J. (2010). *Twitter Power 2.0: How to Dominate Your Market One Tweet at a Time*. Hoboken: John Wiley & Sons, Inc.

Hill, N. (2008). *Think and Grow Rich*. Best Success Books.

Stanley, A. (2003). *Next Generation Leader: 5 Essentials for Those Who Will Shape the Future*. Sisters, OR: Multnomah Publishers, Inc.

iBloom in BUSINESS

Equipping YOU to Build a Successful Business while
Living a Life YOU Love!

For more information about our iBloom in Business
services like the inner circle, one-on-one mentor coaching,
mastermind groups, speaker training, web design services,
copywriting or other resources scan this QR code using
your smart phone or go to www.ibloom.co/business.

Other Ways to Connect with iBloom:

Website – www.ibloom.us
Kelly's Email – kelly@ibloom.us
Facebook – www.facebook.com/ibloomwomen
Twitter – www.twitter.com/ibloom
Pinterest – www.pinterest.com/ibloomwomen

Free Gift for YOU!
One Month FREE in our
iBloom in Business Inner Circle

The iBloom in Business Inner Circle is our way to partner with you and your business, so you can successful implement each step that you've just learned in this book.

Benefits to the Inner Circle include:

- Weekly Video Teachings where we dive deeper into each of the concepts from this book,

- Monthly Q&A Session where you can get answers to your questions, receive accountability, and encouragement,

- Plus, you have the added benefit of encouragement, support, and collaboration opportunities with members in our private Facebook group.

Scan this QR code using your smart phone or go to www.ibloom.co/businessinnercircle to sign-up for the iBloom in Business Inner Circle. Your first month is my gift to you, so I can personally give you accountability and support as you implement all that you've learned. Just use the coupon code: **success** at checkout to receive your discount. This is a month-to-month coaching program, so you can cancel at any time.